BIRMINGHAM
– BUSES –
AT WORK
1913-42

Early days

The first successful motorbuses bought by the Birmingham Motor Express Company (see page 8) were Milnes-Daimler 20hp double-deckers with Milnes O18/16RO bodies. O 264 was the first of the batch of six, and entered service on 12 April 1904 on the route from King Edward VI School in New Street to the Bear Hotel, Bearwood, by way of Broad Street, Five Ways, the Ivy Bush and Hagley Road. On a sunny day in 1904, this pioneering bus, well loaded, especially with adventurous young women on the open top deck, travels though Victoria Square towards Broad Street, with the Head Post Office, designed by Sir Henry Tanner and completed in 1891, in the background. *Author's collection*

BIRMINGHAM
- BUSES -
AT WORK
PART 1: GROWTH, DEVELOPMENT AND WARTIME, 1913-42

David Harvey

FORWARD

·THE NOSTALGIA OF BRITAIN·
from
The NOSTALGIA Collection

First published in 2004

British Library Cataloguing in Publication Data

A catalogue record for this book is available from the British Library.

ISBN 1 85794 237 X

Silver Link Publishing Ltd
The Trundle
Ringstead Road
Great Addington
Kettering
Northants NN14 4BW

Tel/Fax: 01536 330588
email: sales@nostalgiacollection.com
Website: www.nostalgiacollection.com

Printed and bound in Great Britain

ACKNOWLEDGEMENTS

This book would not have been possible without the many photographers whose work is credited within the text. Most of the photographs came from my own archive, but special thanks are due to Peter Drake of the Local Studies Department of the Birmingham Central Reference Library, who allowed me access to their photographic archive, and to Kithead Trust, whose archive material was invaluable. I would like to thank my wife Diana for her proof-reading skills and grammatical expertise, and Derek Potter, whose advice about historical and vehicle details was extremely valuable. Finally, thanks to Peter Townsend of Silver Link Publishing, who, after much cajoling, agreed to publish these two volumes, and Will Adams and Mick Sanders, who had the job of editing and laying out the book.

BIBLIOGRAPHY

The PSV Circle publications about Birmingham City Transport, PD9 and 10, and 2PD2 on the early years of Midland Red, were vital sources of information, as were the BCT vehicle record cards held at the Kithead Trust in Droitwich Spa. The TPC book *Birmingham City Transport* by Malcolm Keeley et al, as well as the two volumes of *Birmingham Corporation* by Paul Collins, were vital, as were the news cutting files held in the Birmingham Central Reference Library and the Transport Committee notes. Finally, the notes made by Barry Ware, augmented many years ago by Peter Jaques, about every Birmingham bus, were of great value and provided the answers to many issues regarding individual vehicles.

CONTENTS

ABBREVIATIONS

ADC	Associated Daimler Co
AEC	Associated Equipment Co
b	built
BaMMOT	Birmingham and Midland Museum of Transport
BCT(&OD)	Birmingham Corporation Tramways (& Omnibus Dept)
BET	British Electric Traction
BMMO	Birmingham & Midland Motor Omnibus (Co)
BRCW	Birmingham Railway Carriage & Wagon (Co)
CBT	City of Birmingham Tramways Co
CMS	Commercial Motor Show
CoF	Certificate of Fitness
EEC	English Electric Co
es	entered service
FEDD	Front Entrance Double Decker
GWR	Great Western Railway
LGOC	London General Omnibus Co
LNWR	London & North Western Railway
LPTB	London Passenger Transport Board
LT	London Transport
MCCW	Metropolitan-Cammell Carriage & Wagon (Co)
MET	Metropolitan Electric Tramways
MoS	Ministry of Supply
MoWT	Ministry of War Transport
NCB	Northern Coach Builders
NCME	Northern Counties Motor & Engineering (Co)
SOS	Shire's Own Specification
TSM	Tilling-Stevens Motors
w	withdrawn

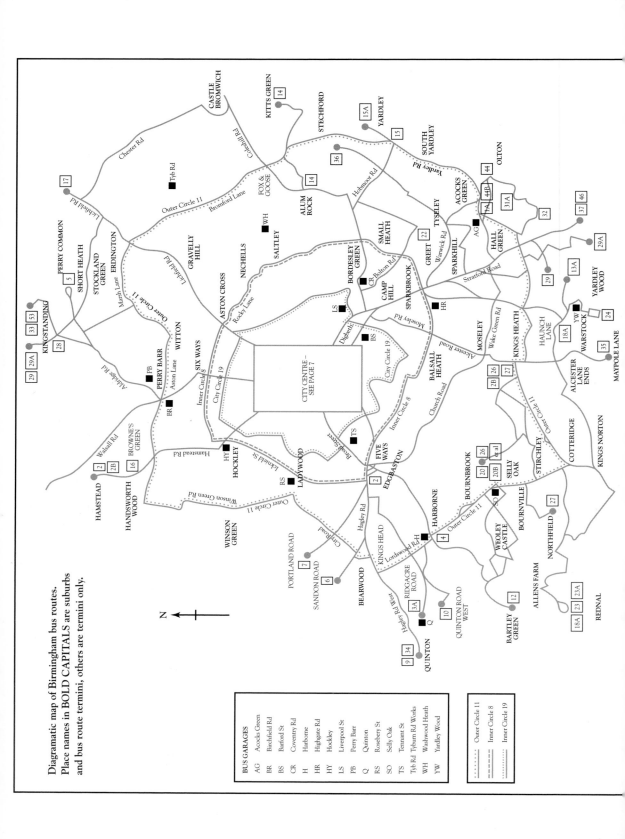

Diagramatic map of Birmingham bus routes.
Place names in BOLD CAPITALS are suburbs
and bus route termini, others are termini only.

BUS GARAGES

AG	Acocks Green
BR	Birchfield Rd
BS	Barford St
CR	Coventry Rd
H	Harborne
HR	Highgate Rd
HY	Hockley
LS	Liverpool St
PB	Perry Barr
Q	Quinton
RS	Rosebery St
SO	Selly Oak
TS	Tennant Sr
Tyb Rd	Tyburn Rd Works
WH	Washwood Heath
YW	Yardley Wood

Outer Circle 11
Inner Circle 8
Inner Circle 19

INTRODUCTION

This is the first of two books looking at Birmingham buses at work, and the aim is to take the reader on a historical journey through time and space, historically and geographically, around the City of Birmingham, using where possible photographs that have not previously been published

Because of the nature of the available material and the types of bus operation, the books describe the individual classes of vehicle chronologically as they entered service, as well as depicting them throughout their working lives. This book starts with the first deliveries of buses new to the then Birmingham Corporation Tramways on 19 July 1913, takes in the buses acquired from Midland

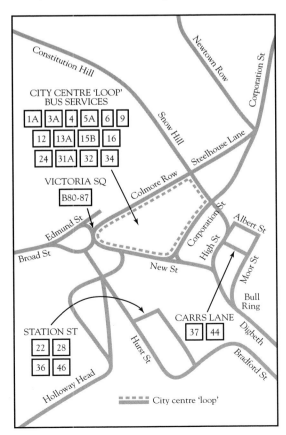

Red on 4 October 1914, and finishes with the last buses built to peacetime standards in 1942.

By looking at Birmingham's buses actually on the road, the book shows the development of the city's motor bus system. Initially buses were used as feeders to the main-road tram services, but gradually the Corporation began to open up bus routes into the new municipal housing estates that were rapidly built around the outer areas of the city. Although tramcars were initially used as the main passenger providers to Acocks Green village, Longbridge, Rednal, Alum Rock, Rubery, Short Heath, Pype Hayes and Hall Green, the last extension was opened on 28 August 1928 to Bordesley Green East, Stechford. After that the bus began to take over the operation of the new extensions beyond the main-road tram routes, so that between 1929 and 1936 new bus services were taking passengers from the City Centre to the new housing estates at Yardley Wood (13), Kingstanding (33), Quinton (3), the Gospel Lane estate in Hall Green (31), Warstock (24), a whole raft of bus routes to Weoley Castle, all numbered 20 plus various letters, Kitts Green (14) and Stechford (36). In addition there was the new City Circle 19 service around the markets area and the Jewellery Quarter, together with the inter-urban service between Northfield and Yardley Wood (18), Kings Heath to Bournbrook (26) or via Bournville to Northfield (27). As well as the service to Sutton Park introduced in April 1933 and a circular bus tour to the Lickey Hills, there were the two cross-city services between Hall Green and Kingstanding (25 and 29), the strange parabolic tour of the city undertaken by the 28 route between Station Street in the City Centre, Small Heath, Washwood Heath and Kingstanding (!), and too many route extensions to mention.

Although there were three early tram route abandonments – the 7 to Nechells, replaced by trolleybuses on 27 November 1922, the 22 Bolton Road route, and the ill-starred 34 along Hagley

Road for a brief period in 1933 – it seemed as though the new Coventry Road trolleybus service to Yardley would be the way forward. However, at that point that the Corporation received a Daimler COG5 bus as a demonstrator, and from 1934 onwards, as a result of the impressive performance of this bus and the early ones of the type that were purchased, the bus reigned supreme in Birmingham. Replacing trackwork and the loss of revenue caused by buses running over the main Stratford Road tram routes were the official reasons for the closure of this group of tram services on 5 January 1937. The two former Company routes to Dudley and the Black Country were closed on 1 April and 30 September 1939 respectively and replaced by buses. Then the Second World War began.

EARLY YEARS BEFORE THE CORPORATION

As early as 1899 a company called the Motor Touring Company applied to run what appears to be little more than a dog-cart between the Fox & Goose at Washwood Heath and Dale End, but although one vehicle was submitted to the Birmingham licensing authorities, it was rejected because of the 'seating arrangements'. On 8 September 1902 a 10-seat Daimler was run for several weeks by Mr W. W. Greener between the steam tram terminus at Salford Bridge and Erdington. The Birmingham Motor Express Co Ltd, formed in early 1903, ran an 18-seat Milnes-Daimler wagonette between the Town Hall and the Plough & Harrow Hotel, Hagley Road, and in June 1903 applied for a licence to run motor buses in the city, although they did not begin until October. Three Napier 12hp vehicles, one single-decker bus and two charabancs all bodied by Mulliner, operated to Fountain Road at the junction of Sandon Road and Hagley Road, and such was the promise of this service that six Milnes-Daimler 20hp 6-seat Milnes-bodied double-deckers were ordered; registered O 264-269, they entered service between New Street and the Bear Hotel, Bearwood, on Tuesday 12 April 1904. In October 1904 O 1270-1275, six Milnes-Daimler 24hp buses, entered service,

followed by three similar vehicles, O 1276-1278, in January 1905. A Thornycroft 24hp demonstrator, O 1279, was loaned from the 'Vanguard' Company of London between March and November 1905, while a German-manufactured Dourkopp, O 1280, and a pair of locally built Wolseley 20hp buses all entered service in February 1905. All were 30-seaters except the Wolseleys, which had a capacity of 36. These were all run on the bus route to Harborne, opened in September 1904. Because of the motorised competition, CBT, which ran the Harborne horse trams, placed in service during May 1905 four further Dourkopp 24hp double-deckers, O 1301-1304.

On 1 June 1905 all the buses were taken over by the newly formed Birmingham & Midland Motor Omnibus Co, whose fleet and operating name was Midland Red. Unfortunately, the summer of 1905 was an extremely hot one, and there were problems with tyres, oil dripping on the road and excessive noise from the Milnes-Daimlers' rack-and-pinion drive. This was the seed for the unfortunate future events, but in the meantime, between October 1906 and January 1907, a further nine Brush B type chassis fitted with 40hp Mutel engines entered service as O 1283-1291. When Midland Red's chief engineer left the company, the expertise and the technical know-how disappeared with him. Increased mechanical and operational problems eventually led to all the surviving motorbuses being taken out of service on 5 October 1907, and by early 1908 all had been sold in a variety of guises as charabancs, double-deckers and single-deckers. Horse bus services were re-introduced on the Harborne service and along Hagley Road, and it was not until 25 April 1912 that Midland Red's first Tilling-Stevens TTA1s re-introduced motorbuses to Hagley Road. These were O 8200-8212, and between February and May 1913 another 24 double-deckers, this time 40hp TTA2s, O 9913-9936, were delivered, so that by September all the Midland Red horse buses were withdrawn. Most of these Tilling-Stevens double-deckers were transferred to BCT on 4 October 1914 and are included in this volume as part of the Corporation's bus fleet.

1.
1913-1922
THE PIONEERING YEARS

Birmingham introduced its first Corporation-operated bus service on 19 July 1913 to Rednal as a feeder for the 35 tram service, which terminated at Chapel Lane, Selly Oak. Ten Daimler CC 40hp buses were introduced, and by 29 November of that year a further route had been introduced to Rubery, just across the Worcestershire boundary. These two services were operated with alternate journeys on a 30-minute headway to each terminus.

The Birmingham Corporation Act of 1914 gave the city full omnibus-operating powers and rights, and on 14 February 1914 an agreement was reached with the Birmingham & Midland Motor Omnibus Company (BMMO) that enabled that company to run over the Corporation's tram routes to and from the city, but prevented it from competing with the Corporation within the city boundary. This was a classic operating agreement, the principles of which formed the basis of many other operating schemes across the country. On 4 October 1914 the Corporation exercised its powers and purchased all the interests of BMMO within the city, taking over 31 Tilling-Stevens petrol-electric double-deckers, the 44-bus-capacity garage in Tennant Street, and six bus routes, including those to Harborne, the Ivy Bush, Moseley and Handsworth Wood. All the buses taken over by the Corporation from BMMO had originally been bought with shares rather than with cash, and were never actually owned by BMMO.

No sooner had this occurred than the War Department made one of its overnight forays and came to Birmingham, giving the Corporation 48 hours to demount the LGOC bodies from the original Daimler CC double-deckers before the chassis were commandeered for military use. The Corporation managed to acquire replacements and also several further batches of buses during the First World War, although they were the later models from both Daimler and Tilling-Stevens. However, despite the new buses there were numerous bus service cut-backs; there was also a shortage of drivers and conductors, as some 2,000 had been enlisted into the military, but it was the shortage of buses that was the main problem. Women conductors were introduced to alleviate staffing problems, but the Corporation bus fleet was constantly being stretched by the increasing demands of the munitions factories in Birmingham, such as the Austin Motor Works at Longbridge. Further cut-backs were caused by national shortages of petrol, especially between May and August 1917, when around 100 merchant ships per month were being sunk by German U-boats.

During the Great War nothing was wasted, with bodies being transferred from one chassis to another, so that by the Armistice in November 1918 the Corporation had a fleet of 52 buses operating on eight main services with several shortworkings on some of them. When the war ended there was a period of consolidation, with only one new bus route opening, to the Stag & Three Horseshoes in Quinton, and no new buses arriving until the forward-control AEC 503 in March 1922. Meanwhile the tram system was still expanding, and already 50 new tramcars, 587-636, had been delivered, but the seeds of the increase in bus services had already been sown and were to alter the transport balance in Birmingham by the end of the 1920s.

1-10 (OA 1601-1610)
Daimler CC; 40hp engine; LGOC
O18/16RO body; b 7.1913, es 19.7.1913

These were the first buses operated by the Corporation and were used as tram feeder vehicles from the Selly Oak tram terminus initially to Rednal on 19 July 1913, then to Rubery

on 29 November 1913. All ten came from a batch of buses ordered by the Metropolitan Electric Tramways Company, which was a BET subsidiary in London. Various numbers are said to have been ordered, but eventually 226 CC types entered service with MET. The Birmingham CCs had chassis numbers that suggest that they were part of the much larger order intended for London but not delivered. All were impressed by the War Department in October 1914.

1 (OA 1601)
Left Still with its paintwork gleaming, the first Birmingham Corporation Tramways motorbus, a virtually new Daimler CC with a London General 34-seat body, is working along Bristol Road South from the Chapel Lane tram terminus of the 35 route towards Rednal, on the city's first Corporation-operated bus service, opened on 19 July 1913. These buses had Daimler sleeve-valve engines built for them by Tylor; running at only 1,000rpm, these were very silent, though perhaps, on account of their valve layout, a bit heavy on lubricating oil. *Author's collection*

5 (OA 1605)
Below Herbert Austin set up his Austin car factory in 1905, and after 5 November 1913 there were two new bus routes to Rednal and Rubery that extended the existing tramway route to Selly Oak. Rather like the Royal Navy, the 'fleet is out' at the junction of Lickey Road, where bus 5 (OA 1605) is parked on the right. There are no locally produced Austin cars in sight as the Longbridge workers leave the factory by either push-bike or on the 'new-fangled' buses. In the background a bus is about to cross the Halesowen branch railway bridge, while on the left, behind the tree, are two more of the LGOC-bodied Daimler CCs working towards Rubery. In all, six of these pre-First World War Daimlers can be seen, all fitted with experimental windscreens. *Author's collection*

7 (OA 1607)
Right The Rubery tramway feeder bus route, first operated on 5 November 1913 by the ten Corporation Daimler CC double-deckers, had its terminus on the forecourt of the ivy-covered New Rose & Crown, which had replaced a previous coaching inn during the mid-Victorian period, some time after the stagecoaches between Birmingham and Bromsgrove had been driven off the road by the Midland Railway's impressive line from Gloucester to Birmingham through the Lickey Hills by way of the fearsome climb of 1 in 37.7 up the Lickey Bank. The driver and conductor pose with their soon to

be commandeered Daimler CC 40hp double-decker outside the inn in the late spring of 1914. *Author's collection*

8 (OA 1608)
Below An over-laden horse and cart, full of barrels and boxes, making its way towards Birmingham, it is about to pass the tree on the corner of Harborne Lane, where the Oak Inn is just visible behind the advertising hoarding for Lemco and Vim cleaning powder. On the right, at the south-east corner of High Street, as this section of Bristol Road through Selly Oak was called, is Oak Tree Lane; it was on this corner that the Old Oak Tree stood, from which Selly

Oak got its name. Becoming diseased during the early years of the reign of Edward VII, the oak was duly felled with much pomp on 22 May 1909. The small gardened island in front of the corner premises of the Ten Acres & Stirchley Co-Operative Society would in later years be replaced by underground public toilets. The as yet unnumbered Selly Oak tram route terminus was at the next junction down the hill towards the city at the Plough & Harrow public house on the corner of High Street and Chapel Lane. Daimler CC 8 (OA 1608) has just left this starting point and is about to cross the junction with Oak Tree Lane on its way to Rednal in the early summer of 1914. *Commercial postcard*

0-12 (O 8200-8212)
Tilling-Stevens TTA1 petrol-electric; Tilling-Stevens 30hp engine; Tilling O18/16RO body; es 5.1912-11.1912; acquired from BMMO 5.10.1914; 7-12 rebodied Brush B25R 1916; w ?.1916-?.1919

These 13 buses entered service between May and November 1912 as part of the BMMO's second attempt to operate motorbuses. Again the Five Ways/Broad Street-Hagley Road/Harborne routes were chosen, as these ran mainly through the Calthorpe Estate's land where electric tramcars were frowned upon by the wealthy householders of the area. These 30hp buses had petrol-electric transmission, which meant that the engine drove a dynamo, which in turn drove the back axle. The buses had a distinctly continental look about them with the radiator being mounted in front of the driver on the bulkhead and a somewhat 'Renault' style of 'coal-scuttle' bonnet. Nearly all the buses were eventually converted to Service Vehicles.

Unidentified 0-12 class
Between 1912 and 1914 BMMO not only began services within Birmingham but also expanded into the Black Country, which quickly became the company's operational heartland. While still being operated by BMMO, this 34-seater TSM stands in Oldbury Market Place behind a hansom cab while waiting to return to Smethwick by way of Langley; the Renault-style bonnet with the radiator mounted at the back of the engine is clearly visible. Within a few months, this bus would be in the ownership of Birmingham Corporation. Behind the railings are the Municipal Buildings, built in 1890 in a stylish red brick, though the rather odd tower somehow isn't 'quite right'. *T. Daniels collection*

4 (O 8204)
'Dear Mother, Fancy me getting to Birmingham by bike, it is 65 miles from here and I lost my way which made me an hour late, yours William.' This is what is written on the back of this evocative postcard of Birmingham's New Street in 1913. While still owned by Midland Red, Tilling-bodied Tilling Stevens TTA1 4 (O 8204) makes its somewhat spindly way along New Street, passing the Colonnade Hotel and the narrow Colonnade Passage on the right where the little horse-drawn van is waiting. The crowds on the right are milling around beneath the canopy of the Theatre Royal, which is starring an actor called James Welch. Further down New Street are a couple of motorcars, a horse bus and, alongside King Edward VI High School for Boys, another of these Tilling-Stevens buses waiting to return to either Harborne or the Kings Head at Bearwood. *Commercial postcard*

13-29 (O 9913-9929)
Tilling-Stevens TTA2 petrol-electric;
Tilling-Stevens 40hp engine;
Tilling O18/16RO body; es 2.1913-5.1913;
acquired from BMMO 5.10.1914;
18 rebodied Brush B25R (1916) in 1924;
w 10.1924-12.1924

The next batch of buses to be ordered by BMMO was 24 of the more powerful TTA2 model. This 40hp-engined TSM again had petrol-electric transmission, but the new front-mounted radiator considerably altered the appearance of these buses, which again were mainly put to work on the Hagley Road and Harborne services. When the Corporation took over the BMMO bus services within its boundary on 4 October 1914, only 17 of these buses were transferred to the municipality.

13 (O 9913)
Above A pair of brand new BMMO-owned Tilling-Stevens TTA2s, led by the first of the batch, stands at the Harborne terminus at the stop near the corner of Serpentine Road in the early spring of 1913. This bus has the original style of radiator header tank badge, whereas the one behind carries the more common 'TILLING-STEVENS' lettering. The second bus is 17 (O 9917), waiting for the crew of No 13 (O 9913) to finish posing for the photographer before driving back to New Street by way of Five Ways and Broad Street. Both buses have a single headlight rather unusually mounted on the canopy above the driver. *Author's collection*

13 (O 9913)
Right On a sunny day during the First World War, No 13 (O 9913) is seen again working on the Rubery service from Selly Oak and Northfield, near Austin's Longbridge factory. Having entered service with BMMO in February 1913, after being taken over by Birmingham Corporation it was employed on the indigenous Bristol Road tram feeder services during the war. The number of buses employed on the former BMMO services was reduced as the demands of war work began to take effect. Meanwhile, the Austin factory's

workforce rose from 2,000 to 20,000, and during the period of hostilities produced more than 2,000 aeroplanes, of which three-quarters were SE5as, 2,500 aero-engines, well over 2,000 2- and 3-ton trucks, numerous turreted armoured cars, 650 field guns and an amazing 8 million shells. So the extra buses were useful! *Author's collection*

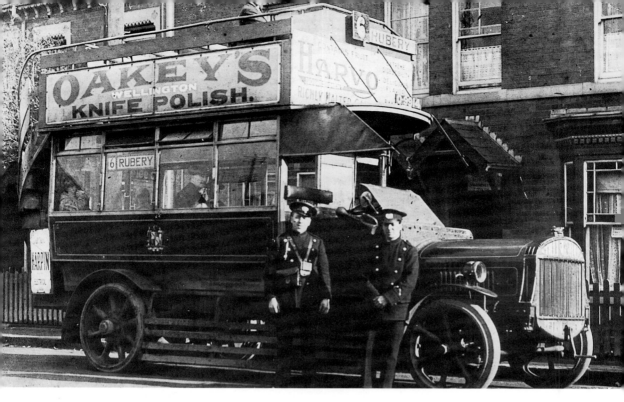

14 (O 9914)

Above By now in Corporation ownership and livery, a very smart-looking bus 14 (O 9914), working on the 6 route to Rubery, stands in Selly Oak alongside some bay-windowed Victorian terraced housing in about 1919. No 14 managed a full 11 years in service, of which 10 were with Birmingham. The petrol-electric transmission made 'crunched' gears a thing of the past; these buses did not have forward gears to change, which made the driver's life considerably easier. In order to give him a little more protection from the elements, the canvas side screen has been 'unfurled'. *Commercial postcard*

18 (O 9918)

Left The Harborne service to Queens Park in Court Oak Road was operated at first as the 'extra', and the main service was the shortworking to Harborne. Bus 18 (O 9918), by now fitted with the later 'Tilling-Stevens Petrol-Electric'-stamped radiator, stands just below the Green Man public house on Harborne Hill. It is operating on the 4 service from the Duke of York public house on the corner of High Street and Lordswood Road, Harborne, and the crew finds time to pose for the photographer despite running to a prescribed timetable. These buses frequently ran against the kerbstones in order to assist the brakes, which could not be relied on when, for instance, descending the steep Harborne Hill. The routes were given numbers when they were taken over from BMMO, and No 18 is operating on the 4 service from the Duke of York public house, which stood on the corner of High Street and Lordswood Road, Harborne. *Commercial postcard*

21 (O 9921)

Right This is a very early view of O 9921, one of the 24 Tilling-Stevens TTA2 double-deckers operated by BMMO, although strangely the vehicles in this batch, numbered O 9920-9936, were on hire from the parent Birmingham District Power & Traction Company and were never actually owned by the operating BET Group company. The bus is standing in Vicarage Road, Langley Green, near Crosswells Road, working on the BMMO service to Blackheath by way of Quinton. Judging by the number of interested children, it could be that it is the first day of operation of this bus service in 1913. *Author's collection*

23 (O 9923)

Below At about the same time that the ten Daimler CC chassis were impressed by the War Department, the Corporation purchased and operated the six BMMO services within the city boundaries. Most of them went either to Harborne or along Hagley Road, but once the Daimlers had gone, the 31 Tilling-Stevens petrol-electrics were also drafted in to work on the two Bristol Road services to Rednal and Rubery. On Wednesday 1 March 1916 the Rednal bus service was given the route number 5 and the Rubery service the number 6, while the shortworking from Selly Oak to Northfield was the 7 and the Longbridge route, which terminated at the Longbridge factory, was to become the 8. On the right, travelling on the newly numbered 5 route to Rednal, is former BMMO Tilling-Stevens TTA2 23 (O 9923), which has come from Selly Oak; rather like an Olympic athlete it looks distinctly out of puff as its radiator steams vigorously as it unloads its passengers at the Bristol Road stop at the corner of Church Lane. Just behind the shops on the right was Victoria Common, which lay undisturbed until well into the 1930s as a reminder of Northfield's recent rural past. The row of shops on the left dates from the 1890s, and standing outside them is another TTA2 working into Selly Oak on the 6 service from Rubery. The impressive wooden bus shelter outside these shops near the corner of Bell Lane was only used for a few years, having gone by the time the tram route was extended to Northfield from Selly Oak on 1 October 1923. *Birmingham Central Reference Library*

24 (O 9924)

Above Queuing up in the shadow of the mock-Tudor splendour of the King Edward VI Grammar School for Boys, completed in 1837 to the designs of Charles Barry and Augustus Pugin, is a row of former BMMO Tilling-Stevens TTA2s. The lead bus is 24 (O 9924), whose top deck is already beginning to look pretty full up with passengers. All the buses are adorned with a front advertisement for 'Sames Pianos', who had a large double-fronted shop in Corporation Street, a sign of the early part of the 20th century when, instead of watching television or even a computer, families would have a musical evening. As a result, Corporation Street could boast four piano-sellers: besides William Sames, there was Cranes & Sons, Scotchers & Son, and Murdoch, Murdoch. A van turns into New Street from Corporation Street, leaving a trail of exhaust smoke among the pedestrians on this warm summer's day in 1914. *Commercial postcard*

26 (O 9926)

Below A lady is about to climb aboard this nine-year-old outside-staircase TTA2 in Harborne High Street in about 1922. No 26 (O 9926) is working on the 4 route, which was taken over from BMMO on 4 October 1914 as a shortworking of the 3 route to Queen's Park in Court Oak Road. The 4 route went to the western end of High Street, Harborne, before turning at the Duke of York public house. It is standing outside the early-19th-century buildings at the corner of Serpentine Road, with Morgan's sweet shop on the corner, where illicit under-age smokers could buy individual Woodbine cigarettes for a farthing. In a few years time, in October 1926, the Corporation's Harborne garage was opened just around the corner in Serpentine Road. On the left is Sadler's newsagent shop, and above the entry is a clock used by the drivers to check their departure times. No 26 was withdrawn in early December 1924, but its Tilling-Stevens body lived on to become a garden house and is now preserved at the BaMMOT bus museum at Wythall, near Birmingham. *Birmingham Central Reference Library*

30 (OA 5711)
Tilling-Stevens TS3 petrol-electric; Dodson O18/16RO body; b 1913; former Tilling demonstrator KT 610; acquired from BMMO 5.10.1914; rebodied Tilling O18/16RO (1912) in 1917; rebodied Dodson O18/15RO (1916) in 1922; w 1926

This bus was fitted with a new type of Dodson body that sat much lower on the chassis frame. The body was called the 'Allen' type, which for many years was wrongly thought to be the name of the body manufacturer.

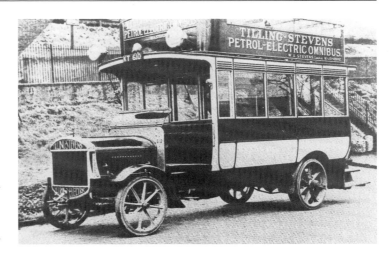

30 (OA 5711)
This official Tilling-Stevens photograph is the only known one of this vehicle. It is in original condition with its first registration mark of KT 610. It had a Dodson 34-seat body that sat lower on the chassis, with the rear wheels actually being inside the rocker panels. In its attempts to sell the bus, Maidstone-based Tilling-Stevens could hardly be accused of being shy about its products. Alas, the body was wrecked in an accident in 1917 and No 30, by now re-registered OA 5711, was fitted with a Tilling body from one of the original 0-12 batch. *Author's collection*

31-40 (OA 1601-1610)
Tilling-Stevens TS3 petrol-electric; es 1.1915; LGOC O18/16RO body (ex-Daimler 1-10), b 1913; 31-38 rebodied Dodson O18/15RO (ex-Daimler Y 41-49) 1922; w 10.1922

These ten chassis were a type exempted from requisition by the War Department, which thought that the petrol-electric transmission was too complicated for war work. As a result, the TS3 became available in the early part of the war. Their bodies, when new, were the ones put into store when the Daimler CCs were commandeered by the Army in October 1914.

33 (OA 1603)
The condition of main roads outside the centre of towns and cities was

frequently awful, as here through what was then the village of Rubery, and had not improved noticeably over the previous half-century despite the increasing demands of motorised transport. Manoeuvring these buses on their solid rubber tyres was difficult enough in the urban centres, where cobbles and sets were a problem to negotiate in the wet. TS3 No 33 (OA 1603), carrying a body from one of the 1-10 class of Daimler CCs, stands in Rubery at the New Rose & Crown public house. When the Corporation acquired ten Tilling-Stevens petrol-electric chassis, it had in store the 1913 bodies from the original 1-10 class of Daimlers, which were fitted to the new war-time deliveries. An intending passenger runs towards the bus just before it is about to leave for the return journey to Selly Oak. *Author's collection*

33 (OA 1603)

Below This posed official BCT view of OA 1603 reveals the new stepped-waistrail Dodson O18/15RO body that was transferred from one of the next batch of Daimler Y types, built in 1916. This second body was just one year newer than the seven-year-old chassis to which it was fitted in October 1922. The location is Somerset Road, Harborne, a favoured spot for such pictures. It will be noted that the TSM chassis were given the registration numbers of the impressed Daimler CCs. This combination remained in service until 1926, when the batch of ten was replaced by new AEC 504 top-covered double-deckers. *BCT*

37 (OA 1607)

Bottom The Harborne bus service had the advantage of not having to compete with a tram service, as the nearest were more than 2 miles away at either Selly Oak (35) or at the Kings Head (34). The only other competition in the area was from the LNWR's Harborne Branch, which had its terminus at Harborne station in Station Road, but competition from the Hagley Road tram service and the increasingly efficient Harborne bus services led to the railway being closed for passenger traffic on 26 November 1934. In about 1920, one of the 1916-vintage TS3s, 37 (OA 1607), still fitted with its first body, built by LGOC for the original 1913 fleet of Daimler CCs, stands in Harborne High Street at the terminus of the 4 route. This was opposite Harborne Park Road near the corner of Serpentine Road, past which the impressive two-wheel horse-drawn carts are trundling on their way into the centre of Harborne. *Author's collection*

– (– —)
Dennis; ? engine; O–/–RO body; demonstrated to BCT ?.1915
No known photograph

– (– —)
Commer Cars; ? engine; O–/–RO; demonstrated to BCT ?.1916
No known photograph

41-46 (OB 1569-1574); 47-49 (OB 2101-2103); 50-52 (OB 2104-2106) Daimler Y; ? engine; Dodson O18/15RO body; es 4.1916-5.1916; rebodied Brush 'K' type O26/20RO 1922; fitted with AEC engines 1925-27; w 1.1927-4.1927

The Daimler Y type was an improved version of the CC model. Production of the new model began in 1916, but was mainly for the use of the Army as lorries. A limited number were allowed to be made available for the civilian market, and Birmingham was originally to have 18, but the last six chassis, allocated numbers 53-58, were impressed by the War Department before delivery.

41 (OB 1569)
The first of the 12 Daimler Y type buses was the subject of an official photograph taken in 1916, when 41 (OB 1569) was new and carrying one of the original rather stylish Dodson O18/15RO bodies. The Corporation was fortunate to obtain these 12 chassis; again, in their early years, they were extensively used on the Longbridge services to the Austin Motor Works, which had become one of the main munitions factories in the city. Although a valuable acquisition, their seating capacity of only 33 was quickly seen as a shortcoming, but it would be well into the second half of their working lives before this was remedied by rebodying the whole batch. *J. H. Taylforth collection*

43 (OB 1571)
Posed in Harborne High Street in about 1922 is one of the rebodied Daimler Y type chassis obtained in April 1916. Bus 43 (OB 1571) is parked next to the early type of Bundy Clock, outside R. J. Davis's florist shop. Next door is the Harborne branch of the Municipal Bank, and these buildings were near to the more westerly of the two junctions with Station Road on High Street and opposite the police station on the corner of Greenfield Road. Bus 43 was rebodied with this straight-sided Brush O26/20R body during 1922, usefully increasing the vehicle's seating capacity by 13. It is working on the 4 route from the Prince's Corner/Duke of York terminus in Harborne towards the City Centre. *Commercial postcard*

47 (OB 2101)

Above As the man smoking the cigarette turns the page of his newspaper, Corporation-owned AEC Y type No 47 (OB 2101) loads up with Austin factory workers in Lickey Road, Longbridge, while working on the Rednal service just after the end of the First World War. The bus is still carrying its original Dodson O18/15RO body, which it will retain for another three years. Meanwhile, an unidentified lorry-bus, ie a lorry chassis with a van body that could be converted to carry passengers, speeds up Lickey Road on its way to Redditch. *Birmingham Central Reference Library*

47 (OB 2101)

Below The same chassis stands on the forecourt of Washwood Heath Depot in November 1923 not long after receiving its new 46-seater Brush body. This garage was used between 1923 and 1925 for motorbus operation, and the buses had to compete for the limited space with the 12 Nechells trolleybuses that occupied rows 7, 8 and 9 on the right-hand side of the depot together with the 50-odd four-wheel Brill-truck class and 71 class tramcars. The bus has been working on the Perry Bar section of what will become the Outer Circle in April 1926. *BCT*

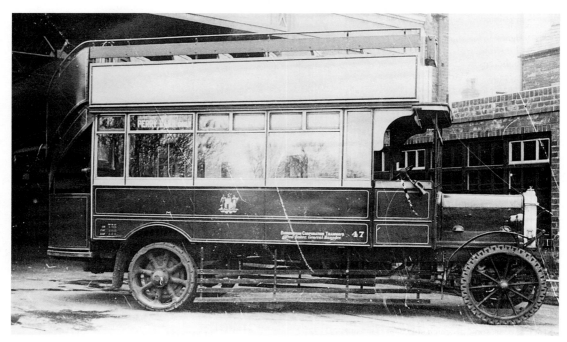

48 (OB 2102)

Above Unloading its passengers in front of the impressive backdrop of Birmingham's Town Hall is rebodied Daimler Y type 48 (OB 2102), which had received its Brush 46-seater body in 1922. Although bigger than the original body, it and the whole bus are still dwarfed by the Corinthian columns of Birmingham's most recognisable building; begun in 1834, it was designed by Joseph Hansom (of hansom cab fame) and was based on the Temple of Castor and Pollux, one of the religious buildings in Rome's Forum. The bus is working on the 4 service from Harborne and will cross the front of Victoria Square and work its way down New Street. These 12 wartime buses were all sold to Southdown Motor Services in 1927, where, once fitted with new AEC petrol engines and pneumatic tyres, they remained in service until the autumn of 1929. *Commercial postcard*

48 (OB 2102)

Right Fairly soon after being rebodied in 1922, all the AEC Y types were fitted with rudimentary windscreens. Bus 48 (OB 2102) stands in Tennant Street near the bus garage, with its capacity for 44 vehicles, that BCT had inherited in October 1914. It had a capacity of 44 buses and actually received some of the first top-covered buses in 1925. When Harborne Garage opened in October 1926, all bus operation was transferred there, but Tennant Street continued as the main works and overhaul base for the bus fleet until Tyburn Road Works was opened in 1929. Although running parallel to the important retail and business quarter along Broad Street, Tennant Street was lined with back-to-back houses and courtyards, some of which survived into the 1960s. *BCT*

53-58 (OB 2107-2112)
Daimler Y; ? engine, b ?.1916

Chassis impressed by the WD before delivery in 1916.

53-58 (OB 2107-2112)
Tilling-Stevens TS3; Tilling engine; Tilling O18/16RO body (1912, ex-0-12); es 4.1916; 54-58 rebodied Brush B25R (1916) in 1919; w 9.1926-9.1929

The development of feeder bus routes with light passenger loadings led to five of these six wartime double-decker TSM TS3s being rebodied with new Brush B25R bodies after three years.

54 (OB 2108)

Below This Tilling-Stevens TS3 bus was rebodied in 1919 with a body that had originally been fitted to the underpowered former BMMO TSM TTA1 No 7 (O 8207) in

1916. The rear-entrance Brush bodywork was characterised by having unusually deep saloon windows. No 54 (OB 2108) stands in Harborne posing for a series of official photographs; in this guise it remained in service until 1928. *BCT*

57 (OB 2111)

Below left The statue of Joseph Sturge, the eminent Victorian philanthropist, was unveiled on 4 June 1862 some three years after his death. He was a Quaker who made his fortune by trading in corn, but then used his fortune to campaign against slavery. Bus 57 (OB 2111) is in its original state, fitted with a Tilling double-deck body that was originally on one of the 'Renault'-bonneted Tilling-Stevens TTA1s of 1912 inherited from BMMO. It is working on the 1 route from Moseley in about 1919 and stands alongside the statue at Five Ways, which at that time stood between Calthorpe Road, from where the bus has emerged, and, on the extreme left, the start of Hagley Road. It will continue into the City centre by travelling straight on into Broad Street. Five Ways was the first major intersection on the roads leading out of the city to the west. Although Broad Street never had trams, Five Ways had two tram routes running across it, both coming from Islington Row on the right. Passing in front of the Five Ways public house on the corner of Broad Street and Ladywood Road are the overhead wires for the 33 tram route to Ladywood. The tram tracks that bus 57 has just crossed are those for the 34 route along Hagley Road to the Kings Head at Bearwood; this had the unfortunate distinction of being the first main-road route to be abandoned on 11 August 1930 after a relatively short and unpopular life of only 17 years. *J. Whybrow collection*

57 (OB 2111)

By now rebodied as a single-decker, No 57 (OB 2111) stands in Colmore Row facing Snow Hill station. This was when Colmore Row was a two-way street, something that would not be altered until the infamous one-way traffic system was inaugurated on 5 June 1933 and immediately made Birmingham the butt of many a music-hall comedian's jokes in much the same way as the myths about 'Flying Dutchmen' motorists on the never-ending present-day M25 motorway. The bus is parked outside Barclays Bank opposite the entrance to Temple Row. The railings of St Phillip's Cathedral are on the extreme right, while straight on are the piano and musical instrument showrooms of W. H. Priestley & Sons at 71-73 Colmore Row. *Birmingham Central Reference Library*

59 (OK 3980)
AEC 503; AEC 6.8-litre engine;
Fry O28/26RO body; es 2.1922; w 1927

This was an AEC demonstrator, originally built as a 403 type chassis, between 26 February and 26 March 1922, and was purchased in the latter month. It was Birmingham's first new post-war double-decker and, although still an open-topper, the first vehicle to have a forward-control layout.

59 (OK 3980)

The AEC 503 model was introduced in 1922 and was basically a more powerfully engined AEC S type, of which 928 were being supplied to LGOC. No 59 (OK 3980) was the first of just 15 of the 503 model supplied to Birmingham Corporation, and was the first of the second generation of double-deckers that it bought, culminating with the last of the ADC 507 chassis entering service in 1929. The bus had bodywork by Fry, a company based in Greenwich that supplied a number of bodies for the 148 503 types built between 1922 and 1925. This bus, unlike many of the succeeding AEC 503s and 504s, was fitted with a windscreen. Despite its ground-breaking appearance, No 59 was withdrawn in 1927 and sold for further service to Cumberland Motor Services as its No 80. *BCT*

– (XH 9629)
Tilling-Stevens TS3; Tilling engine;
Tilling O28/22RO body

Demonstrated to BCT between 11 March and 1 April 1922, there is no known photograph of this vehicle.

– (TB 8886)
Leyland SG7; Leyland engine;
? O22/20RO body

Demonstrated to BCT between 3 April and May 1922, there is no known photograph of this vehicle.

2.
1923-1928
EXPANSION INTO THE SUBURBS

After the end of the Great War, the tramcar in Birmingham reigned supreme, basically because motorbuses still lagged behind in terms of reliability, speed, passenger capacity, comfort and economy. Buses were open-topped, had outside staircases and ran on solid rubber tyres, while the trams, being totally enclosed, carrying more passengers and running on pairs of four-wheel bogies, were a far more sophisticated method of carrying the public. However, as early as 26 November 1922 the first closure of an electric tram route, that to Nechells, took place. The trams were replaced by a fleet of 12 Railless trolleybuses, which pioneered enclosed upper decks, a feature that BCT would quickly adapt to the double-deck motorbus fleet. Despite this pioneering trolleybus service, in Birmingham this alternative method of electric public transport was little more than a footnote in the change-over from tram to bus, which almost insidiously overtook the somewhat traditional-looking tramcar.

After first using a small number of single-decker motorbuses to connect with tram routes, the first half-cab forward-control double-deckers were purchased. The domination by AEC of Birmingham's orders throughout the 1920s was because of the development of that company's new models. Beginning with the 503 model, the succeeding 504s and 507s became more and more sophisticated: covered top decks, pneumatic tyres and enclosed drivers' cabs were introduced as this generation of buses gradually became the workhorses of the rapidly increasing bus system. Ten new bus services from the City Centre into the suburbs were introduced during this period, as well as the famous Outer Circle 11 and Inner Circle 8 routes and the extension of existing ones.

1-8 (72-79) (OK 5484-5491)
Leyland A1; Leyland S3 24hp engine;
Buckingham B20F body; es 12.1922-
1.1923; renumbered 72-79 3.1923;
w 9.1929-12.1931

These small single-deck buses were designed to be used as one-man-operated vehicles for lightly used outer-suburban services and tramway feeder routes. They were introduced with solid rubber tyres but were quickly converted to become among the first buses in Birmingham to operate on pneumatics.

2 (73) (OK 5485)
Soon to be renumbered 73, OK 5485 stands in Harborne opposite the Duke of York public house at the top of War Lane's steep hill. These buses were operated as one-man vehicles, so the gentleman leaning on the headlight with the cash bag and ticket machine, who looks like the conductor, is in fact the driver. Birmingham-based bodybuilder John Buckingham produced eight attractive-looking bodies mounted on the 2-ton Leyland A1 chassis. The buses were given pneumatic tyres within a year of entering service, thus dating this posed picture to 1923. The large front-mounted destination box is incorrectly showing the route number 11, but the bus is actually working on the 12 route, introduced on 29 January 1923 between Harborne and Bartley Green, as displayed on the side box. *Author's collection*

– (TC 2128)
Leyland SG7 Special; Leyland S5 40hp petrol engine; Dodson O28/26RO body; b 1922

Leyland Motors tried to gain the Birmingham double-deck order that was being proposed for 1923, and demonstrated this vehicle to BCT between 20 January and February 1923. The bus featured equally sized front and rear wheel rims at 850 mm, and carried a Dodson body constructed with an open-top body style that was beginning to find favour with London's independent bus operators.

– (TC 2128)

The 1 route, which ran from New Street to Moseley Village by way of Broad Street and Five Ways, was taken over from BMMO on 5 October 1914 and was renumbered from its original 9 route number on 1 March 1916. TC 2128 was the latest SG7 Special model from Leyland Motors, but it was unsuccessful in obtaining an order. It was the first 'semi-forward'-control Leyland double-decker and had a rather ugly distinguishing 11-inch-long 'snout'. It is standing in Salisbury Road with its conductor apparently posing

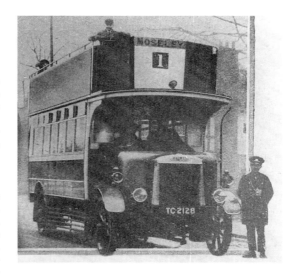

alongside the nearside front wing, although there are genuine passengers on the open upper deck. *Author's collection*

60 (OK 6364)
AEC 403; AEC engine; ? B32F body; b 1923

Demonstrated to BCT from 27 March to 12 May 1923, it was renumbered 80, but has no known photograph.

61 (NO 6856)
AEC 403; AEC engine; Dodson B32D body; b 1923

Also demonstrated to BCT from 27 March to 12 May 1923, it was renumbered 81, but has no known photograph.

–/63/– (DH 1456, 1903, 1905)
Dennis-Stevens TS3; Dennis engine; Dodson B28F body; es 1919-20 as Walsall Corporation 22, 27 and 29

These three buses were briefly on loan from Walsall in February 1923 due to a temporary shortage of buses.

20 (DH 1454)

Although no pictures of this trio have come to light, this similar Walsall Corporation Motors motorbus, 20 (DH 1454), a Dennis-Stevens petrol-electric bus with a Dodson B28F body, is seen standing in the middle of Walsall prior to undertaking a private hire. Note that the men are standing outside in 'organising pose' while the women sensibly sit in the bus. The bus was quite advanced for its day, boasting electric lighting, but with a body design

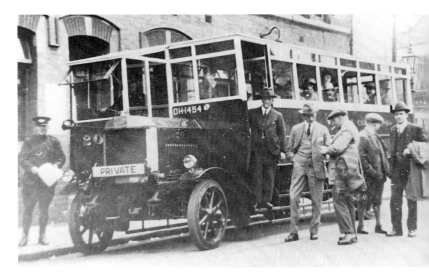

that almost required crampons to mount the steps leading to the saloon. *Author's collection*

– (– —)
Tilling-Stevens TS-; Tilling-Stevens 35hp petrol-electric; ? B34- body; b 1923

Demonstrated to BCT in about June 1923, there is no known photograph of this vehicle.

60-71 (OK 8002-8013); 89-90 (OK 8014-8015)
AEC 503; AEC 6.8-litre petrol engine; Brush O28/26RO body; es 4.1923-7.1923, w 6.1927-9.1930

The 15 Birmingham AEC 503s, including the Fry-bodied 59 (OK 3980), were the first production examples of this new chassis, which had been developed as a larger-engined version of the LGOC S type and its 'provincial' equivalent, the 403 series, from which all Birmingham's 503 chassis were converted prior to completion. They began Birmingham's association with AEC, which lasted for nearly ten years. No 62 was fitted with the prototype top-cover for double-deckers between July and September 1924.

Unidentified 60-71/89-90 class
Below An unidentified bus is peeking out of Icknield Street as it waits to cross Spring Hill during the early days of the still incomplete Inner Circle 8 bus route. These open-topped buses ran for all of their seven years on solid rubber tyres and

were also never top-covered, except for the experiments with 62. This was just as well, as in this case they were able to get underneath the low bridges in Icknield Street and Highgate Road. To the right of the bus, in Summerhill Road, is the Palace Theatre, originally been opened as a variety theatre in 1905, becoming a cinema just six years later. Towering over the bus is the ecclesiastically styled Spring Hill Library, opened in 1893. It was built in a Gothic revival style with an almost excess of terracotta brickwork, and was an 'oasis of culture' among the unsanitary back-to-back houses and courtyards that spread out in a desert of Victorian urbanised squalor. *Birmingham Central Reference Library*

62 (OK 8004)
Below left This was the first AEC 503 chassis, and the first Birmingham motorbus, to be fitted with a top-cover, at Kyotts Lake Works in July 1924, after 15 months' service. Although the top covering of any double-decker vehicle was frowned upon because of the inherent instability caused by the extra weight, Birmingham was at the forefront of the practice, initially with the tramcar fleet but also with the 1-12 class of Railless F12 trolleybuses introduced on the Nechells route on 27 November 1922. No 62 (OK 8004) stands in the works on 11 July 1924, where its design was used as a model for Brush, which built the first production top-covered motorbus on 101 (qv). No 62 was never operated in this condition, which perhaps is just as well, as some of the plate glass came from Tilling-Stevens TTA2 17 (O 9917) and still bore the etched number plate of that vehicle. *Author's collection*

62 (OK 8004)

Right Travelling away from Five Ways along the arboreal Harborne Road and crossing the Highfield Road junction on 20 May 1926 is bus 62 (OK 8004). Built with a Brush body, it was experimentally fitted with a top cover in July 1923; it never ran in service in this condition, and quickly reverted to its original open-top cover. However, within months bus 101 (OL 8100), the first of the AEC 504s, was delivered from Brush with a fitted top cover looking remarkably like that fitted to 62. The bus is working on the 3 route, a service inherited from the BMMO company on 5 October 1914. Harborne Road was part of the Calthorpe Estate centred around the western suburb of Edgbaston, which had, and still has, some of the most prestigious housing in the city. These buses were instrumental

in the early operation of the Inner Circle bus route, being, in their open-top condition, the only ones capable of getting beneath Icknield Street and Highgate Road railway bridges; the driver had to stop the bus while the conductor climbed the stairs to request that passengers remain seated until the bus had cleared the bridge. *Birmingham Central Reference Library*

66 (OK 8008)

Below During the General Strike, Birmingham Corporation's employees followed the official TUC line and between 5 and 11 May 1926 the Corporation's trams, trolleybuses and buses were generally prevented from leaving their depots and garages, although volunteer bus drivers, many of them students from the University of Birmingham, managed to get a few of the buses on to some routes. Standing at the head of a queue of buses in High Street, Harborne, at the corner of Serpentine Road, is No 66 (OK 8008); a policeman looks on as two men give the driver some last-minute instruction before the bus sets out for Birmingham on the 4 route. *Author's collection*

80 (OK 9852)
Daimler CK2; Daimler 22hp sleeve-valve engine; Buckingham B21F body; es 6.1923, w 11.1931

These small buses were introduced as one-man-operated vehicles for outer-suburban services and tramway feeder routes. This was at a time when the large municipal housing

estates in Short Heath, Pype Hayes and Kingstanding were being rapidly developed and before the decision was made to extend existing tram routes, as occurred in Stechford, or introduce newer and eventually larger buses.

80 (OK 9852)
This first Daimler CK2 was the only one with a Buckingham 21-seater body. Looking slightly shorter than the eight later

Daimler CK2s, No 80 (OK 9852) is parked outside Fondella's confectionery and tea rooms in Reservoir Road working on the 11 service; this had been extended from Erdington to Stockland Green on 16 July 1923, then on 12 November 1923 it was extended through Witton to Perry Barr. It was operated by these small single-deckers between Acocks Green and Perry Barr for the next 14 months, dating this photograph to 1924. Behind the bus is Wilkins chemist shop on the corner of Slade Road, the first shop in the terrace of retail outlets that marked Stockland Green's shopping centre. *N. C. Meacham*

81-88 (OL 1714-1721)
Daimler CK2; Daimler 22hp sleeve-valve engine; Strachan & Brown B24F body; es 10.1923-11/1923, w 9.1929-9.1930

These eight buses were also introduced as one-man-operated vehicles for outer-suburban services and tramway feeder

routes. These were among the first buses in the country to be fitted with pneumatic tyres, early in 1924.

82 (OL 1715)
In the summer of 1925 bus 82 (OL 1715), the second of the Strachan & Brown-bodied Daimler CK2s, is at the top of Marsh Hill alongside the impressive-looking Stockland Inn,

opened on the previous 24 November. By this time the penultimate extension of the 11 bus route had taken place, taking it from the Kings Head on Hagley Road through Winson Green, Perry Barr, Erdington and on through Stechford to Acocks Green. Although the complete encircling of the city by the 11 route would not take place until Wednesday 7 April 1926, it was, after the February 1925 extension to Bearwood, known as the 'Outer Circle'. On the left is one of the MRCW-bodied 637-661 class of bogie trams, which had entered service towards the end of 1923. It is standing at the Stockland Green terminus of the 1 tram route, which would be extended as the 78 route on 23 June 1926, only 2½ months after the 11 bus service finally enclosed the city. *Author's collection*

83 (OL 1716)

This closer view of 83 (OL 1716), as it stands at the exit of Harborne Garage, shows what neat little buses these 24-seaters were. The first three rows at the front were for smokers, who were separated from the rest of the passengers by a glass and wooden partition. The buses were placed on pneumatic tyres within months of their delivery, but such was their success in their role of opening up new routes that their small seating capacity became a handicap. Harborne Garage had opened on 12 October 1926 with a capacity for 100 buses and was the first purpose-built bus garage built by the Transport Department. It replaced the former BMMO garage in Tennant Street, though that remained opened as the bus repair works until Tyburn Road Works opened in December 1929. *BCT*

B104, 465, 611, 1150, 1561, 1734, 2295, 2456, 2531, 4971, 5091 (LN 4804/7101/ 223, LE 9933, LF 8337/ 8504/8903/9584/9637, LH 8437/8590) AEC B type; AEC engine; LGOC O18/16RO body; on hire from LGOC 6-7.1925-10.1925

These buses were used on the pre-Outer Circle service to augment the hard-pressed Leyland A1 and Daimler CK2 single-deckers until new double-deckers were delivered. There are no known photographs of them.

B1124 (LE 9920)

No known photographs exist of the 11 AEC B type double-deck buses that were hired from London General to supplement the little single-deckers operating on the infant Outer Circle service, and they lasted only until there were sufficient new buses available for an all-day service on the 11 route. B1124 (LE 9920), seen with its conductor and driver posing for posterity at Twickenham, is numerically close to those used in Birmingham and is of the same body type as those operated in the city. *Author's collection*

101 (OL 8100)
AEC 504; AEC 5-type 6.8-litre petrol engine; Brush H26/24RO body; es 7.1924, w 4.1935

This was one of the most important buses to enter service in Britain, let alone Birmingham! It was the first motorbus in the

city to have a top-cover for the upper saloon from new (remember that experiments with the 15-month-old bus 62 had begun just two weeks earlier), although for its first few weeks in service it retained the original design without a peak over the front windows. This was altered within a few weeks of entering service in order to fit a front ventilator in the upper saloon. The driver sat in an open cab with a metal cowling for usual protection and a tarpaulin cape to protect him in the event of rain or snow. The reason for all future Birmingham double-deckers being top-covered was that, during inclement weather, passengers who would previously have tried to squeeze into the lower saloon for shelter, could now stay dry and the bus could realise its full revenue potential in the wet.

101 (OL 8100)

Ironically, after being involved in the development work for Birmingham's top-covered double-deckers, Brush was to body just one of the 107 AEC 504s supplied to the Corporation. By putting No 101 (OL 8100) into service on 24 July 1924, the Corporation was able to take advantage of Birmingham City Police's more lenient interpretation of the requirements for operation. Coupled with the AEC 504 chassis's quite wide track, this bus was the first in the country to have a top-cover mounted on a forward-control chassis, beating London General's AEC NS types by just over a year. Yet again, the supposedly staid image of Birmingham Tramways department has been totally disproved with the adoption of top-covers on all double-deckers from this time. No 101 stands in School Road, Yardley Wood, in late July 1924. BCT

102-131 (OM 201-230)
AEC 504; AEC 5-type 6.8-litre petrol engine; Short H26/26RO body; es 11.1924-1.1925, w 11.1934-7.1936

This was the first production batch of 30 top-covered AEC 504 buses in the fleet, but the body contract went to Short Brothers, which was still fairly new to the bus-bodybuilding

industry. Shorts was a seaplane manufacturer and made its first bus body in 1919, but with re-armament in the mid-1930s producing a full aeroplane order book, the company pulled out of producing bus bodies towards the end of 1935. Birmingham placed most of its orders for double-deck bodies with Shorts between 1924 and 1930, and it was during this period that the city, with Shorts' assistance, began to seriously experiment with metal-framed bodywork. This first batch enabled full use of the vehicles' seating capacity in inclement weather. The upper saloon was finished in blue leather and the lower saloon cushions were covered in blue moquette. Both saloons were equipped with electric lighting.

108 (OM 207)

No 108 (OM 207) is travelling along Yardley Road, Acocks Green, through the rather well-to-do late-Victorian residential area on the 11 route on 13 June 1934. All the 504s were converted to run on pneumatic tyres after 1927, and during subsequent overhaul they were rebuilt to 507 standard by the substitution of pressed-steel chassis members that superseded the weaker, flitched construction. It is in this condition that 108 has left the Coventry Road junction at the Swan public house and, having just crossed the bridge over the Birmingham & Warwick Canal, opened in 1799, makes the sharp turn at Dalston Road. Once at the top of the next rise, the bus will cross the railway bridge at Acocks Green station, on the GWR's main line between Birmingham's Snow Hill station and Paddington, London. Ironically, while the outside-staircase AEC/ADC 504 and 507 family of buses were the pioneer double-deckers on the Outer Circle route, the same route gave them their last regular employment. The sizeable house to the left of the bus stood next to the canal and guarded the entrance to the large sand and gravel pits that were located alongside it. *Birmingham Central Reference Library*

115 (OM 214)

The bus is working on the 1 route from Moseley towards the city centre on 18 August 1925, and is waiting at the junction of Priory Road, Edgbaston, with Bristol Road, which was where Birmingham's first traffic lights were installed during 1929. This area of Edgbaston marked the edge of the Calthorpe Estate, which was well-known for its tree-lined roads and large detached houses such as the one on the right, which is dwarfing both the tree and the bus. Bus 115 (OM 214) is about seven months old and is still on solid rubber tyres. The driver has his weather-proof tarpaulin covering him, while the distant policeman on point duty is wearing his white traffic duty coat. *Birmingham Central Reference Library*

132-161 (OM 9546-9575)
AEC 504; AEC 5-type 6.8-litre petrol engine; Short H26/26RO body; b 9.1925-11.1925, w 12.1934-7.1937

This was a further batch of 30 Short-bodied 504 chassis purchased for the further expansion of existing services, and were virtually the same as the first batch. Most of these 30 buses were used to develop new services and to increase frequency on existing ones.

146 (OM 9560)

The driver of OM 9560, which entered service on 9 October 1925, poses for the photographer while a cloche-hatted woman looks on curiously from the lower saloon. As the bus is still equipped with solid rubber tyres and the 6 service from the City Centre loop along Broad Street and Hagley Road to the Sandon Road terminus outside the Birmingham Municipal Bank on the corner of Willow Avenue was not opened until 29 September 1926, it is fairly safe to assume that this posed picture was taken at about that time. The method of tying the tarpaulin weathershield is well shown here, the top piece being attached to hooks located on the driver's canopy. When the driver re-entered his cab, he would attach the side piece to the bulkhead, in the manner of a cab door. Just over the driver's shoulder are a pair of brass fire extinguishers and the rather splendid bulb for the horn. The shield coming down from the driver's canopy could be used as either a rain deflector or sun visor. *A. N. G. Glover*

154 (OM 9568)

No 154 (OM 9568) travels up the hill in the tree-lined dual-carriageway of Harborne Park Road near Vivian Road during 1932, working on the 11 route and travelling towards Harborne. Nearly 200 top-covered AEC 504s were in service by the time the Outer Circle service was completed, enabling Birmingham's passengers to have a dry ride in the upper saloon, while elsewhere in the country contemporary top-covered buses were still in the experimental stage. Harborne Park Road was converted into a dual-carriageway in 1926 in readiness for the new 11 bus service, but was also to be part of the 'Grand Plan' to have wide, tree-lined roads with central reservations encircling the city. Throughout the inter-war years, sections of roads on an anti-clockwise arc from Hagley Road around to Witton were completed, but certain pieces were destined never to be remodelled, while the rest of the route through Perry Barr, Handsworth and Winson Green had an already well-established Victorian road system that was unsuitable for conversion. To the right, on the corner of St Peter's Road, is the famous Harborne Cricket & Hockey Club, formed in 1868 and moved to the Old Church Avenue site in 1874. *Birmingham Central Reference Library*

162-171 (ON 1313-1322)
AEC 504; AEC 5-type 6.8-litre petrol engine; Short H26/26RO body; es 12.1925, w 12.1934-7.1937

This was another batch of 10 Short composite-bodied AEC 504s for use on the new services to Yardley Wood and the completion, on 7 April 1926, of the 11 Outer Circle route.

167 (ON 1318)

Speeding along College Road on 22 May 1933, No 167 (ON 1318) appears to be empty, as it is not on the 5 route, the number it is showing. Almost certainly the bus is working back to its base at Perry Barr Garage, and has just crossed the Tame Valley Canal, which joined the Birmingham & Fazeley Canal at Salford Bridge. The shop in the distance, to the right of the bus, stands at the junction of Kingstanding Road on the left and the continuation of College Road. On the right is a Cleveland petrol station, although on this Monday it is not being patronised as there appear to be no passing motorists. *Birmingham Central Reference Library*

– (ON 1125)
AEC 507; AEC 5-type 6.8-litre petrol
engine; Short H28/22RO body; b 11.1925

This bus was the first AEC 507 chassis; it was exhibited at the 1925 Olympia Commercial Motor Show in full BCT livery, and was demonstrated to BCT in November 1925. It went to Doncaster Corporation as No 53 in October 1926.

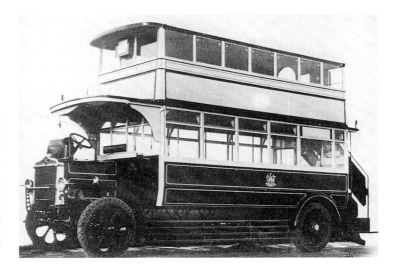

– (ON 1125)
This publicity photograph was taken for the 1925 Olympia Show, and shows the full Birmingham specification Short body. The 507 chassis differed from its predecessor by having a pressed-steel construction rather than the flitched version that had been used on the old 504 model. The 507 was also one of the first chassis to be given a name by AEC, though in this case the name 'Ramillies' was not often used. *AEC*

29 (ON 5400)
AEC 504; AEC 5-type 6.8-litre petrol
engine; Brush B26R body (b 1916);
b 4.1926, w 1936

The reason for the purchase of this bus is something of a mystery as it was a double-decker chassis that received the 1916 Brush B25F body that had started life on No 8 (O 8208), one of the 1912 Tilling-Stevens TTA1s inherited from Midland Red. The body was then put on 1916 Tilling-Stevens TS3 No 55 (OB 2109) during 1919, where it remained until 1926. After barely a year in passenger service it was used as a driver trainer. In June 1931 it was converted into a dual-control trainer and used until February 1936.

29 (ON 5400)
Being used as an instruction vehicle, having recently been converted to a dual-control trainer on 8 July 1931, single-deck AEC 504 No 29 (ON 5400) travels through Northfield with the driving instructor, armed with suitable foot pedals, an enormous handbrake but no steering-wheel, sitting behind the trainee driver. The only other known picture of this bus is in a film taken in Harborne Garage in 1927, which shows No 29 in its original condition with an open half-cab and protective cowl, so the full front must have been added when the bus was converted to a dual-control trainer.
Newspaper cutting, author's collection

172-191 (OP 201-220)
AEC 504; AEC 5-type 6.8-litre petrol engine; Short H26/26RO body; es 9.1926-10.1926, w 6.1934-8.1936

This was another batch of the by-now standard Short-bodied AEC 504s, again purchased to augment the increasingly pressurised bus fleet. Strangely, this was quite a short-lived batch, only two surviving into 1936.

176 (OP 205)

Below A good deal of the northern and eastern parts of the completed Outer Circle 11 bus route was still open countryside when it finally encircled the city on 7 April 1926. Loading up with passengers in Stechford Lane, No 176 (OP 205) is on its way towards Stechford, Yardley and Acocks Green. This AEC 504 had another of the standard wooden-framed Short H26/26RO bodies, and entered service on 1 September 1926. Buses like this really began to

open up the new routes that were beyond the limits of the tramcar services; although nominally limited to 20mph, they became the workhorses of the Corporation's bus fleet until the introduction of the revolutionary AEC 'Regents' at the end of 1929. Their conversion to pneumatic tyres at the end of the 1920s enabled them to continue to provide a valuable role until they were finally swept away by the introduction of the vast numbers of Daimler COG5s during the mid-1930s. Behind the bus is the recently reconstructed Fox & Goose public house and the wide open spaces of the yet to be developed Bromford Lane. *J. Whybrow*

179 (OP 208)

Below Being waved out of New Street and into Victoria Square by the policeman on point duty in about 1928, No 179 (OP 208) is working on the 4 service to the Duke of York, Harborne. The bus is following a three-wheeler cyclecar, which appears to be a CWS, constructed by the Co-op

movement in Tyseley, Birmingham. Towering above the bus is the Head Post Office building on the corner of Pinfold Street, designed by Sir Henry Tanner and completed in 1891. On the left is Christ Church Buildings, better known as Galloway's Corner, which was built on the site of the woodworm-ridden Christ Church in 1899. *Commercial postcard*

192-201 (OP 221-230)
AEC 504; AEC 5-type 6.8-litre petrol engine; Thompson H26/26RO body; es 10.1926-2.1927, w 11.1934-7.1937

Thompson was a small coachbuilder based in Louth in Lincolnshire, and successfully tendered for these ten bodies on the BCT standard AEC 504 chassis.

193 (OP 222)

Above The tram tracks outside St Phillip's Cathedral in Colmore Row were used by the Corporation's Handsworth

199 (OP 228)

Right By the time OP 228 travelled along Sherborne Road, Acocks Green, on 13 June 1934, it had been running on pneumatic tyres for several years; these would at least give a fairly smooth ride while the road surface is being replaced. The bus has just left Acocks Green Village and will shortly arrive at the GWR's Acocks Green station. With its 6.8-litre petrol engine, the AEC 504 was capable of about 4mpg, and once put on pneumatic tyres was easily capable of 35mph. This part of Acocks Green had distinctly superior villa-type houses, such as those behind the trees on the right and three-storey terraces on the left, and was well served by public transport: the 11 route linked the suburbs by bus, the 44 tram route went to Albert Street in the City Centre, and of course there were the train services to the other suburban stations in Birmingham as well as further afield.
Birmingham Central Reference Library

tram routes; on the alignment of the CBT cable cars, they would remain operational for the electric trams until 4 June 1933, when the termini for Handsworth tramcar routes were moved into nearby Livery Street. This was caused by the extension of the one-way street system into Colmore Row, which would make it impossible for traffic to travel towards Snow Hill station from Victoria Square; OP 222 is doing so in about 1928 while working on the 9 service, introduced on 31 March 1919 to serve the Quinton area to the west of the city centre via Hagley Road. This rear view of the bus shows the outside staircase arrangement with the well-protected entrance to the upper saloon. *Commercial postcard*

202-207 (OP 231-236)
AEC 504; AEC 5-type 6.8-litre petrol engine; Buckingham H26/26RO body; es 9.1926, w 3.1935-8.1936

John Buckingham's coachbuilding factory was located at 332-333 Bradford Street, Birmingham, and after a promising few years of supplying buses to railway companies and local Midlands operators, it became a victim of the Depression. This was the company's first double-deck contract for the Corporation, mounted on the last batch of AEC 504 chassis.

204 (OP 204)

The driver and an inspector talk with the conductor at the back of No 204 (OP 204) while working on the Outer Circle 11 route. The bus is standing at the Bundy Clock in Lordswood Road alongside the wooden fence that protected the crown green of the King's Head's bowling club. It is quite late in the bus's career, as it is operating on pneumatic tyres. Other than that modification, the appearance of the bus has hardly changed since it entered service in September 1926. As well as the open staircase, 204 has an open cab; it is said than many of the drivers preferred the open cabs to the enclosed ones found on the later 507 model, because the latter leaked and became steamed up in the rain. *Author's collection*

207 (OP 236)

The impressive municipal buildings in Victoria Square made even double-deckers look like toy buses. The last six AEC 504s to be delivered to BCT&OD were bodied by Buckingham, and No 207 (OP 236) loads up with passengers outside Lyons Corner House in the Christ Church Buildings block when working on the 4 route to Harborne. On the opposite side of the square, behind the statue of Queen Victoria, erected in 1901, and, to its left, one of her son, King Edward VII, erected in 1913, is the soot-encrusted facade of Birmingham's Council House. This had been designed by Yeoville Thomason (1826-1901), whose bold and eclectic competition-winning design in a romantically classic style took four years to build. It was finally opened in 1878 with much ceremony and high Victorian pomp. *Commercial postcard*

208 (OP 237)
Guy BKX six-wheeler; Daimler-Knight 6-cylinder 7.672-litre petrol engine; Short H32/26R body; es 11.1926, w 12.1933

This was an early example of the Guy six-wheeled family of chassis, which had been introduced earlier in 1926. This normal-control double-decker was displayed at an exhibition in Liverpool in November 1926, and the original chassis was replaced by Guy Motors in 1927. This was the last normal-control double-decker to be delivered, but was the first to have an enclosed staircase.

208 (OP 237)

Birmingham Corporation, despite its apparently somewhat staid image, was always at the forefront of trying out new types of buses. This impressive beast is 208 (OP 208), a Guy BKX with a very thirsty Daimler 7.672-litre sleeve-valve engine. It was mounted on pneumatic tyres from new and was the first Birmingham double-decker bus to have an enclosed cab. Its Short H32/26R body had for the first time the capacity of a top-covered tramcar. It had an enclosed staircase, but wasn't the first vehicle to have this feature, as the experimental EMB trolleybus 13 (OL 4636) of 1924 was similarly equipped. No photographs have come to light of this bus in service, probably because of its unreliability, but when it was new it was extensively photographed in Metchley Lane, Harborne, for Birmingham official publicity purposes. Weighing in at 6 tons 11 cwt 3 quarters, this leviathan was nearly a ton heavier than the standard AEC 504. It spent the whole of its life working from Harborne Garage, and although it was taken out of service at the end of 1933, amazingly the body survived as a holiday retreat and is now part of the Aston Manor Transport Museum Collection. *BCT*

209 (OP 238)
Karrier DD6 six-wheeler; Dorman 6JUL 6.9-litre petrol engine; Short H32/28R body; es 8.1927, w 11.1929

This was a large forward-control six-wheel double-deck chassis with double-drive to the rear axles. It was fitted with an enclosed driver's cab and rear platform and staircase, but the chassis was very heavy, underpowered and unreliable, especially regarding the drive shafts and back axles. Its unreliability caused it to be withdrawn after only two years PSV service, and it

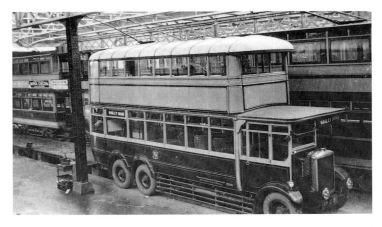

became Service Vehicle 15 in May 1931 as a breakdown crane lorry until January 1938, when it was replaced by AEC 'Renown' 663 (MV 489).

209 (OP 238)

Again there are apparently no photographs of 209 operating as a bus, but the Karrier DD6 was photographed inside Selly Oak Garage and Tram Depot in about 1928. It is parked over the pits alongside some of Selly Oak's allocation of four-wheeled 301 class open-balcony cars, and is visibly comparable in size to these 29ft 3in trams. The totally enclosed cab, with its rather ornate cab door handle, projects in front of the upper saloon, which still manages to contain 32 seats. No 209 (OP 209) has been operating on the Hagley Road service, beyond the Kings Head 34 tram route terminus, to Quinton. *A. D. Packer*

210-219 (OP 3650-3659)
AEC 507; AEC 5-type 6.8-litre petrol engine; Buckingham H26/26RO body;

es 2.1927-3.1927, w 3.1932 (burned out)-8.1936

These were the first of the steel-chassis-framed AEC 507s to be purchased. The Buckingham bodies were the last class to be delivered with open cabs, but this batch of ten buses were the first double-deckers to be delivered with pneumatic tyres.

210 (OP 3650)

The 1 service to Moseley was operated by outside-staircase buses from 1924 until the withdrawal of Acocks Green Garage's last AEC 504/507 buses. No 210 (OP 3650) was the first of the new 507 chassis type to be delivered to the undertaking, and is loading up with passengers at the Five Ways bus stop in Calthorpe Road before travelling along Calthorpe Road towards Priory Road in about 1929. The building to the left of the bus is the neo-classical Portland stone frontage of Lloyds Bank, completed in 1909 to the design of P. B. Chatwin. The tree-lined Calthorpe Road had numerous early-19th-century detached villas built in a classical early-Victorian Gothic style. *Author's collection*

220-234 (OP 7863-7877)★; 235-244 (OX 1501-1510)★★
ADC 507; AEC 5-type 6.8-litre petrol engine; Short L20/26RO body; b 6.1927★, 10.1927-11.1927★★, w 10.1933-5.1934

Two batches of these low-height buses were purchased to operate specifically on the new Inner Circle 8 route, which was completed as a ring on 8 February 1928, although three-quarters of the circle had been operating from Saltley to Hockley by way of Five Ways since 16 August 1926. This class of 25 buses had only 20 seats in the upper saloon arranged in a herringbone fashion on a central raised section, which allowed the lower saloon gangway to have a full-height ceiling; this arrangement led to the nickname of 'pickpocket specials'. The Inner Circle route had 14ft 3in railway bridges at Icknield Street, Hockley, and Highgate Road, Balsall Heath. and required low-height enclosed top-deck buses.

225 (OP 7868)

This splendid view over the body shop in Tyburn Road Works was taken in 1930, just after the introduction of the first of the 'piano-front' AEC 'Regents'. This was in the days when skilled labour was still cheap: there are 37 mechanics and body-makers in the workshop, which resembles more of a factory than a bus repair works. On the left is low-height bus 225 (OP 7868); this class was very poorly recorded on film, so two in one picture is a rare treat! Careful examination shows that the upper saloon seats have been removed, revealing the raised centre section on which the seats were arranged in echelons. The earlier 1927 batch also had the strange little cubby-hole extension at the rear next to the outside staircase. Alongside 225 is the withdrawn 63 (OK 8005), an open-top Brush-bodied AEC 503, while in the centre is 290 (VP 1154), one of the 1928 group of ten low-height buses. The next bus to the right is 296 (VP 1160), with a normal-height Shorts body. On the right is 146 (OM 9560), an AEC 504 with a Short body dating from 1925. *Author's collection*

229 (OP 7872)

When viewed from the nearside, the lowbridge Short bodies gave the impression of having enclosed staircases, but they were outside. No 229 (OP 7872) is seen at Short Brothers' factory on about 1 June 1927; the 'pickpocket specials' were rarely photographed in service. They were the first buses to be equipped with roof-mounted front destination boxes with roller blinds; these were not a great success and most were replaced with the more normal between-decks route box. When they were new these low-height buses revolutionised the Inner Circle service, and this official view shows that the AEC 507 chassis were delivered with pneumatic tyres and were the first buses to have the driver's cab enclosed on an half-cab double-decker. No 229 was one of the first to be withdrawn after the accident illustrated below in August 1933, when it had its roof ripped off in Sandy Lane when it was just six years old. *Author's collection*

245-259 (OX 1511-1525) AEC 507; AEC 5-type 6.8-litre petrol engine; Short H26/26RO body; es 9.1927-10.1927, w 3.1935-6.1937

These buses were the first high-bridge forward-control double-deckers to have an enclosed half-cab. Again they were 52-seaters with outside staircases. They were also the first buses to incorporate a roof-mounted destination box.

259 (OX 1525)

Displaying the slip-board for 'OUTER CIRCLE' on the radiator header tank, 259 (OX 1525) waits outside the Bull's Head in Stechford on a sunny day during the summer of 1934, about a year before it was withdrawn. It had been operating on pneumatic tyres for about five years, giving its passengers a more comfortable ride and its many drivers a much easier life! The bus had just crossed Stechford Bridge over the River Cole and its frequently waterlogged flood plain. The bridge was near to Stechford Mill, which was one of 16 on the Cole used either as grist-mills or adapted to provide water power for industry.

The huge Bull's Head was built at the beginning of the 20th century, replacing an earlier Georgian building on the corner of Station Road and Flaxley Road. The Edwardian replacement was built in a strange mixture of styles, combining Tudor half-timbering with wings in a mullion-windowed Jacobean design. *J. E. Cull*

260-274 (OX 1536-1550)
ADC 507; AEC 5-type 6.8-litre petrol engine; Buckingham H26/26RO body; es 9.1927-10.1927, w 4.1935-7.1937

The final order received by Buckingham's was for 15 composite bodies on the ADC 507 chassis. By 1927 the standard Birmingham body was a quite advanced double-decker, especially when compared with other operators' contemporary buses.

270 (OX 1546)

The 13A bus route was first operated on 5 June 1929, so when No 507 accelerated past the impressive portico of Birmingham's Council House in August 1929 the extended service to School Road, Yardley Wood, was still something of a novelty. Behind Victoria Square's ornate silver-painted gas-lights, the passengers on 270's top deck have opened the windows to their maximum three-quarter drop position, allowing for a fairly cool and comfortable run from Yardley Wood's council estate, which had been set around the wide open spaces of Billesley Common and the River Cole valley near the remains of the once thriving slit mill at Trittiford. The bus is about to leave Victoria Square and pass along Colmore Row on its way towards St Phillip's Cathedral, a manoeuvre made impossible by Birmingham's first one-way-street scheme of 5 June 1933. The bodies on the 507s would still have looked antiquated when compared to newer buses even if the panelling-over of the lower saloon cant-rail ventilators had taken place. *G. H. F. Atkins*

272 (OX 1548)

Still running on rubber tyres, 272 (OX 1548) negotiates the traffic island at the junction of Coldbath Lane and Brook Lane, into which it is turning. On the left is the Billesley Hotel, opened in 1927 and for many years claiming to being the largest public house in the city. It replaced a much older structure that looked more like a farmhouse than a hostelry. The bus is working on the increasingly busy, recently completed Outer Circle route in about 1929, when turns like this at a traffic island, with a full load of passengers, were arm-wrenching for the poor driver. Bus drivers from about this time until well into the 1960s were frequently penalised by insurance companies; all the steering wheel pulling, especially on buses with solid rubber tyres, caused strain on the pectoral muscles, and also the heart, and increased the insurance risk! *Commercial postcard*

275-284 (OX 1526-1535)
ADC 507; AEC 5-type
6.8-litre petrol engine;
Vickers H26/26RO body;
es 10.1927-11.1927,
w 5.1935-6.1937

The only batch of motorbus bodies built by Vickers for the Corporation were on this batch of ten ADC 507s. Vickers, based at Crayford, Surrey, made a brief success of manufacturing bus bodies at a time when, like Shorts, the company experienced a lull in aeroplane orders.

276 (OX 1527)

The development of Corporation Street began in the late 1870s as part of Joseph Chamberlain's 'Grand Plan' for a 'Parisian Boulevard'. By the end of the century, the street was lined with high-Renaissance-style Flemish-inspired buildings and was the equal of any provincial city's shopping area. Besides the bus, most of the remaining traffic consists of outward-bound tramcars on the 10 and 3X routes and a virtually new Midland Red single-decker, which enables the well-dressed pedestrians to walk fairly freely almost as though it was the semi-pedestrianised street of the present day. OX 1527 is about to cross the tram tracks coming out of Martineau Street in about 1929, and is working on the 13A service, displaying the wooden radiator destination board 'YARDLEY WOOD'. The original brackets for these destination boards can be seen on the leading edge of the canopy above the enclosed driver's cab. *Author's collection*

285 (OX 1570)
AEC 507; AEC 5-type
6.8-litre petrol engine;
Short H24/26RO body;
es 9.1927, w 6.1937

This bus was the first in the fleet to have a prototype all-metal alloy-framed body. Despite its modern construction, the body's design was curiously old-fashioned and would not have looked out of place on the earlier 504 chassis. It also had the by now obsolete open cab in front of the first body to be delivered with flush-sided panels without a rocker panel.

285 (OX 1570)

Apart from official Short Brothers' photographs taken when 285 was new, the only other picture of this quite revolutionary all-metal-bodied bus was taken outside the brand new Selly Oak Tramway Depot and Bus Garage. These premises came into use on 12 July 1927, so OX 1570, still with its pneumatic tyres deeply treaded, must be only a few weeks old. It is showing the incorrectly mixed-up destination 5, which was to Perry Common, while the 7 route was to 'PORTLAND ROAD', which was a cross-city service that had been coupled with the 5 route from its inception on 26 September 1927, just two days after 285 entered service. The photograph also reveals that both the 5 and 7 routes must have been worked by the new Selly Oak premises for a short while before being transferred to the year-old Harborne Garage. Only 12 open-cab buses would survive beyond 285's withdrawal in June 1937, and they only lasted for another month. *Author's collection*

286 (OX 4594)
ADC 802; Daimler CV35 Mk I 5.7-litre petrol engine; Short FH36/32R body; b ?.1928; Associated Daimler Co demonstrator 30.1.1928-28.10.1928; renumbered 100 7.1928

The ADC 802 was a six-wheeled bus designed for, but operated without enthusiasm by, the London General Omnibus Company as its London Six model. LGOC had 12 examples, and the other eight were either used as unsuccessful demonstrators or as staff transport by the parent AEC company.

286 (OX 4594)
Again, there are only official Short Brothers' photographs of OX 4594, taken in Rochester alongside the River Medway, this 29-foot-long leviathan dwarfing the Austin Seven standing beside it. The bus was fitted with an all-metal body with enclosed staircase, and was perhaps the best looking of all the 802s, having a top deck resembling those on the later AEC 'Renown' 663s of General's LT class. The whole effect was somewhat spoiled by the lower saloon's clerestory windows and the 'shed' that purported to be the full-width, totally enclosed driver's cab. The bus was garaged initially at Acocks Green, although it was seen operating from Harborne Garage during its unsuccessful nine-month loan period, during which it only worked from January to June and ran a niggardly 7,886 miles, suggesting that mechanically all was not well; in March and April it only averaged about 500 miles per month, against the normal 3,000. The 'London Six' was renumbered 100 in July 1928, but apparently never ran in service with this fleet number. The trial was terminated in accordance with ADC's letter of 28 October 1928. *Short Brothers*

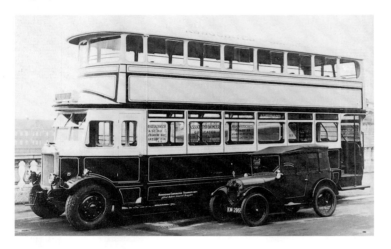

– (TE 1128)
Leyland 'Titanic' TT1; Leyland 6.8-litre petrol engine; Leyland H40/32RO body; b 1927

This six-wheel version of the Leyland 'Titan' was a Leyland Motors demonstrator. TE 1128 was operated from Harborne Garage for its period of demonstration during 1928.

– (TE 1128)
Waiting at the Lonsdale Road entrance to Harborne Garage is unnumbered demonstrator TE 1128. A shaft of light comes through the glass in the garage's Belfast roof and illuminates the front of the bus sufficiently to reveal that it is about to leave on another circuit of the Outer Circle 11 route. This huge six-wheeler with the unfortunate model name 'Titanic' did not enjoy many plaudits with the re-engineering staff as problems with the rear bogie springs and the final double drive did not endear the bus to the undertaking. TE 1128 was the first of only six TT1s to be built, and was sold by the end of 1928 to Midland of Airdrie, Scotland, which ran it on the arduous 87-mile run between Glasgow and the Irish package port of Stranraer for the next 18 years, so it couldn't have been all that bad! *Author's collection*

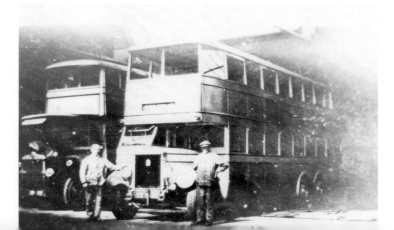

286-295 (VP 1150-1159)
ADC 507; AEC 5-type
6.8-litre petrol engine;
Short L20/26RO body;
es 8.1928, w 8.1933-6.1934

These were the final batch of lowbridge buses for the Inner Circle bus route. Like the previous batch, they had half-drop lower saloon windows, obviating the need for the tram-like clerestory cant-rail ventilator windows. Together with the longer upper saloon overhang over the driver's cab and the overhanging 'cupboard' over the rear platform, giving the conductor some extra protection, this gave the illusion of a much more modern vehicle than many of its contemporaries. It was only when aboard that the awkwardness of the design was noticeable: the lower saloon had an arched roof on top of which were mounted the herringbone upper saloon single bucket seats with two side gangways. These buses, like the earlier ones nicknamed 'pickpocket specials', had a short life, being replaced when the less lofty Daimler COG5s were introduced.

287 (VP 1151)

Top right The final ten ADC 507s were slightly different from the 1927 examples. They had full-depth opening upper saloon windows to improve ventilation, but the front-dome-mounted destination boxes were replaced with the old-style destination number box. When Aston Villa was playing at home, all available Corporation trams and buses were brought into service, including any spare low-height buses, which were largely based at Barford Street Garage. Here a queue of buses waits in Jardine Road, which linked Witton Road and Trinity Road on the western side of Villa Park and was a useful parking spot before the fans poured out of the ground. No 287 (VP 1151) stands at the front of a row of four other earlier low-height buses, the second and third from the 220-244 batch of 1927; the third one still retains the roof-mounted front destination blind box. At the back of the queue are four of the 1923 batch of open-top AEC 503s. *Author's collection*

289 (VP 1153)

Above right On Monday 3 March 1930 this bus managed to decapitate itself when working on the recently extended 13A route from Yardley Wood. There was an official diversion in the Camp Hill area of Stratford Road to avoid some roadworks, but the driver managed to get lost in Henley Street and was directed by a policeman into Sandy Lane, where there was a 12ft 6in bridge – this was the result! The picture reveals the two upper saloon side gangways and the single bucket seats arranged in echelon down the centre. The basic body is still intact, and 289 (VP 1153) was returned to service, surviving until mid-June 1934, when all the remaining lowbridge ADC 507s were withdrawn. On the peeled-back ceiling can be seen the centrally mounted bulkhead light, while the broken front destination number box hangs drunkenly above the rear platform. Amazingly, only two passengers were injured. Members of the Transport Department look on, and even from the rear have a look of incredulity about them as they survey the wrecked bus. *Author's collection*

296-337 (VP 1160-1201)
ADC 507; AEC 5-type 6.8-litre petrol engine; Short H24/26RO body; es 10.1928-3.1929; w 5.1937-7.1937

These 42 buses were the last high-chassis, outside-staircase buses to be delivered. The Short bodies were metal-framed and could easily be distinguished by having shallower upper saloon windows with full-depth sliding windows. The new method of construction enabled the unladen weight to be reduced by 7 cwt to 5 tons 7 cwt, but the waist-rail height was raised by several inches, which always gave the bodies on this final class of ADCs a somewhat perched look!

301 (VP 1165)

Top The municipal housing estates that straddled the Acocks Green/Hall Green boundary were built in the late 1920s, and on 24 September 1930 the 31 service was introduced, going from Lakey Lane towards Olton Boulevard East and operated by Acocks Green Garage, which opened in June 1928. No 301 (VP 1165) is in Gospel Lane at the compulsory stop about halfway around the Gospel Lane 'Loop' in 1932, by which time the municipal terraced houses on this large residential development were only a few years old. Although some of the old field trees were retained, staked saplings were planted to increase the greenery alongside the carriageways, as seen here. *Author's collection*

308 (VP 1172)

Middle The driver and conductor proudly pose in front of bus 308 (VP 1172), working the 30 route to Olton. In the background is the Acocks Green & Olton Laundry, located at the end of some large Edwardian villa-style housing on the steep hill along Warwick Road from Culham Close towards Lincoln Road. In fact, the 30 terminated at the junction of Warwick Road and the newly constructed Olton Boulevard East. These last ADC 507s were obsolete within a year, when the then ultra-modern AEC 'Regent' 661s were introduced with their low-framed chassis and inside staircase. The 507s had full-depth sliding upper saloon windows to improve passenger comfort, but were still recognisably an early 1920s design. All were gone by 1937. *J. Whybrow*

318 (VP 1182)

Bottom Pulling away from the penultimate bus stop in Highfield Road, Hall Green, on 22 July 1931, is 2½-year-old bus 318 (VP 1182), working on the 29 route towards the almost invisible terminus near Yardley Wood railway station. Tree-lined suburbia should have been the preserve of the tram, as in cities like Liverpool, Sheffield and Glasgow, but in Birmingham the buses gradually and insidiously dominated the trams, and it was the bus routes along Stratford Road and beyond the tram lines to reach the outer-city housing estates that really put paid to that group of tram routes. The existing tram route had been extended by about three-quarters of a mile to the city boundary at Hall Green from opposite Highfield Road on 2 April 1928, the penultimate route to be lengthened, but changing transport requirements conspired to end the short life of this reserved-section tramway. The 29 bus service was first operated on 6 February 1928, initially as a cross-city service to the Boars Head public house at Aldridge Road, but later to the Kingstanding Circle. In the 1920s the policy was that dual carriageways such as Highfield Road's central reservation were built to take tram tracks if required at a future date, but the rapid improvements to the bus fleet meant that this policy was never carried out, which is why the young lady on the left, on her way home to her almost new three-bedroomed semi-detached house, has got off a bus, not a tram. *Birmingham Central Reference Library*

3.
1929–1933
LATEST TECHNOLOGY AND
SUPPORT FOR LOCAL INDUSTRY

The year 1929 presaged change. The last major tram extensions had taken place during the previous year, while the penultimate Birmingham tramcar, the Short Brothers lightweight car 842, had entered service in November 1929. Between 1930 and 1934 the tram system saw the abandonment of the Bolton Road, Hagley Road and Coventry Road routes, while a short extension along Holly Lane from Tyburn Road into the Fort Dunlop complex was opened as the 63 route on 13 February 1930. Throughout this period, however, ten new bus services were introduced, mainly into the new Corporation housing areas, such as Kingstanding, Warstock, Perry Common, Weoley Castle and Glebe Farm. By the end of 1931 28 bus routes were advertised in Kelly's Directory, but there were still 48 tram routes. However, the bus was already in the ascendancy. In addition, the City Circle 19 route through the inner-city slums, the markets area and the Jewellery Quarter was opened on 2 March 1932. Meanwhile many existing bus routes were extended towards the city boundaries, where people from the inner-city back-to-back slums were being re-housed on new Council-built and owned housing estates.

This was also a period of great contrasts. In March 1929 the last of the old generation of chassis, the ADC 507, entered service, and although fitted with pneumatic tyres, a metal-framed, totally enclosed top deck, and a driver's cab, the body still had an outside staircase and three deep steps into the lower saloon. Then, on 18 October 1929, Birmingham's first AEC 'Regent' 338 (OF 3970), the tenth to be built, was 'made available for service', and at a stroke made everything that had gone before obsolete! Various body-makers such as Brush, Vulcan, English Electric, Short and Metro-Cammell built their interpretation of the BCT-specified 'piano front' body until 1932, when orders for AECs stopped. The Metro-Cammell order was one of the earliest and was so successful that the company's metal-framed bodies became the preferred choice for the Corporation over the rest of the undertaking's existence, which ended in 1969. The dominance of AEC finished towards the end of 1930 when the local unemployment needs of the Depression years forced the City Council to encourage the Transport Committee and the General Manager, A. C. Baker, to support local industry.

Although many vehicles were demonstrated to the Corporation at this time, including buses with the still fairly new oil or diesel engine, the initial batches of locally manufactured buses came from an unlikely source. The Morris-Commercial company had only just left Smethwick for the newly created Adderley Park factory, and was trying to break into the large PSV market with a range of models that included the double-deck 'Imperial' and the single-deck 'Dictator'. With names like those, no wonder they didn't sell! However, together with the Metro-Cammell all-metal body developed by the Saltley-based company, here was the answer to Birmingham's problems, both politically and operationally. One cannot accuse Birmingham of not trying – of the 83 Morris-Commercial 'Imperials' built, the city operated 51 of them. The post-Depression years meant that, where possible, many operators attempted to support their local industry, such as Manchester Corporation's support for Crossley

Motors, and Birmingham thought that, with Morris, it had fulfilled its aim. Unfortunately, the Morris-Commercial chassis were mechanically not up to the job and another answer had to be found.

The impending opening of the Coventry Road trolleybus route in January 1934 and the ordering of 50 Leyland TTBD2 six-wheeled trolleybuses with Metro-Cammell 58-seat bodies and GEC electrics seemed initially to be the way forward, as at least two of the components, the bodies and the

electrics, were made locally. Then in November 1933 the Corporation discovered the fluid flywheel and Wilson pre-selector gearbox when a Daimler demonstrator was tried out, but this time with the fuel-efficient Gardner 5LW diesel oil engine. Almost at the finishing line, when the trolleybus was about to be introduced with great success, the Corporation had found a locally manufactured motorbus that was so good that the excuse to use a locally built bus chassis was no longer needed!

99 (OF 3959)
Leyland 'Titan' TD1; Leyland 6.8-litre petrol engine; Leyland L24/24R body; b 12.1928, w 2.1935, to Preston Corporation (60), 1935

This Leyland Motors demonstrator entered service on 8 January 1929 with the Short H26/26RO body from AEC 504

No 159 (OM 9573), with which body and fleet number it ran until June 1929. A replacement chassis was supplied in August 1929 and a new Leyland L24/24R lowbridge body, its upper saloon featuring a sunken offside gangway and alternate rows of three and four seats across the centre and nearside, enabling passengers and conductor to manoeuvre when the top deck was full; this combination returned to service on 29 September 1929 as 99. In February 1932 the bus was purchased and fitted with a Leyland 8.1-litre diesel engine in July 1932.

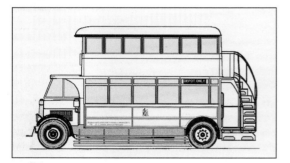

159 (OM 9573)
Left A drawing giving an excellent idea of what the original TD1 demonstrator chassis 159 (OM 9573) must have looked like when running with the outside-staircase Short body. The body had to be modified around the front bulkhead, rear wheel arches, the bottom steps of the staircase and the rear platform, producing an ungainly looking hybrid. Interestingly, there are no mileage records for this bus when it was operating with this body. *A. T. Condie*

99 (OF 3959)
Below left This official BCT photograph, taken in September 1929, shows the enclosed rear staircase and platform of this 48-seat lowbridge bus with its side gangway on the top deck. Enclosed staircases on Leyland bodies had only been in production since the summer of 1929, so 99 (OF 3959) was quite advanced for its date. It was also unusual for a Leyland in that it did not carry a spare wheel under the staircase, which was the standard procedure for Birmingham. At first sight, the reason for the purchase of this lowbridge bus is surprising, but it was seen as a possible successor to the low-height 'pickpocket special' ADC 507s and was operated by Barford Street Garage, although initially it was allocated to Harborne. In this condition it worked around 3,000 miles per month, amassing just over 180,000 miles by the time it was sold to Preston Corporation. *BCT*

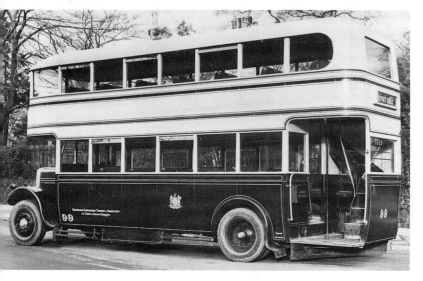

99 (OF 3959)

Small Heath in the 1930s was a very mixed urban landscape; the inner part was heavily industrialised with large tracts of unsanitary back-to-back, terraced and courtyard properties interspersed with the factories. Along Coventry Road, away from nearby Grange Road, the quality of the housing improved dramatically, with large 1860s Victorian terraced houses, such as those beyond Golden Hillock Road, from which the lowbridge ADC 507 'pickpocket special' is emerging on the 8 route. Careful examination of the overhead wires in this 1934 view reveals that trolleybuses have taken over from trams along Coventry Road; the recently abandoned tram lines are about to be crossed by a Ford Model A van, while a Midland Red Brush-bodied SOS QL of 1928 follows a line of large cars towards the city. Having come out of Muntz Street while working on the outer, clockwise ring of the Inner Circle route is No 99, which by this time had a Leyland oil engine and Leyland 48-seat lowbridge body; whatever the disadvantages of the latter, it did enable the bus to pass beneath the low bridges in Icknield Street and Highgate Road, but although the drivers apparently liked it, it was very unpopular with both conductors and passengers alike. It was also the last bus to be delivered in the mid-1920s corporate colours with the elaborate blue livery lines and gold lining. *J. Whybrow*

– (MT 2114)
AEC 'Regent' 661; AEC
7.4-litre petrol engine;
Short H26/24RO body;
b 2/1929

G. J. Rackham's move from Leyland Motors back to AEC as Chief Engineer in 1928, where he designed the 'Titan' TD and 'Tiger' TS models, led to his new 'Regent' double-decker and 'Regal' single-decker designs, updated versions of his radically designed chassis first introduced by Leyland. MT 2114 was the prototype 661, chassis number 661.001, fitted with a Short Brothers 50-seater body. It was a measure of how important Birmingham was as a customer that the prototype was kept as an AEC demonstrator for a fortnight in March 1929. There had been a long-standing Masonic affiliation between Birmingham's first two General Managers, Alfred Baker and Arthur Chantry Baker, and members of the AEC senior management, which considerably enhanced AEC's ability to continue gaining large orders for buses after the introduction of this new model. The prototype's successful visit led to the 'Regent' becoming the standard Birmingham chassis for the next three years, during which time the Corporation purchased 159 chassis, and just one bus from another manufacturer!

– (MT 2114)

The only known photographs of the prototype MT 2114 while being demonstrated to the Transport Department are a set posed in front of a typical 'Bayco building set'-styled 1920s detached house in suburban Birmingham. In its demonstration livery of off-white and red bands, it stayed on loan from 4 to 18 March 1929, running a total of 2,091 miles in service on the Inner Circle 8 route. The Short Brothers outside-staircase body looked like a lowbridge bus from the ground, but in fact had a 'camel' hump running above the central upper saloon gangway, thus making it unsuitable for the low bridges on the Inner Circle service! *Author's collection*

97 (UK 8047)
Guy 'Invincible' FC; Guy 7.672-litre petrol engine; Hall Lewis H24/24R body; b ?.1929

The Guy 'Invincible' FC double-decker was not a very common chassis, but was the first of numerous unsuccessful attempts by the Wolverhampton-based manufacturer to obtain orders from Birmingham. No 97 was a Guy Motors demonstrator, borrowed from December 1929, although it was periodically returned to Guy for modification, including fitting it with a Gardner 6LW 8.4 diesel engine in 1932. It was returned again on 18 January 1934 for the 6LW engine to be fitted into the 'Arab' FD chassis, which became 208 (OC 8208). The body was demounted to survive as a hulk for several months, then was probably broken up, although BCT records suggest that parts of it could have been used in assembling the replacement 'Arab' chassis.

97 (UK 8047)
The impressive chateau-styled six-storey Midland Hotel on the corner of Stephenson Street and Lower Temple Street was part of the original 1875 Birmingham Improvement Scheme. On the ground-level corner site is the 'CAFÉ' sign for the Birmingham Coffee House, while to the left of the bus is the car showroom of George Heath, agent for the Rootes Group and Daimler. The Guy 'Invincible' demonstrator 97 (UK 8047) pulls away from its stop at the Queen's Hotel end of Navigation Street on the 30 service to the junction of Olton Boulevard and Warwick Road. This service was replaced on 24 September 1930 when it was extended as the 31 service into the Gospel Lane municipal housing estate. *R. Marshall*

97 (UK 8047)
On a sunny day in Paradise Street in 1932, bus 97 (UK 8047) pulls away from the bus stop outside the ornate brick and terracotta Tudor-styled street frontage of Queen's College Chambers; built in 1843 as an Anglican Training College, its façade was rebuilt in 1904. Directly opposite the bus is the entrance to Ratcliff Place, alongside Birmingham's Town Hall. The Guy is working on the 3 route to Queens Park in Court Oak Road, Harborne, and has by this date been fitted with the Gardner 6LW diesel engine, which might account for the cloud of smoke it is leaving. The 3 route was one of the former BMMO routes taken over by the Corporation on 5 October 1914. Travelling into the city from Harborne is AEC 'Regent' 661 No 496 (OV 4496), which had a Metro-Cammell metal-framed body and was one of the last 20 of this successful model to be purchased, entering service on New Year's Day 1932. *Author's collection*

51-60 (OF 3960-3969)
Guy 'Conquest' C; Guy 7.672-litre petrol engine; Guy B26F body; es 9.1929, w 5.1935-1.1936

These ten buses were impressive-looking normal-control single-deckers, originally bought for use as one-man-operated vehicles on lightly loaded suburban services, replacing the eight-year-old Daimler CK2 and Leyland A1 20-seater single-deckers. Unfortunately, the Board of Trade placed a limit of 20 seated passengers, standing being prohibited on single-deckers operated by only the driver. Although this body could seat a few more, it was uneconomic to work such large-engined, small-capacity buses with a crew of two, yet they were frequently too small for the increasing number of passengers. All ten were returned to Guy Motors during October/November 1931, the chassis lengthened and the body converted to forward-control B32F.

58 (OF 3967)

Top The Birmingham & Fazeley Canal was one of many built to the design and route-line of John Smeaton; completed in 1790, it passed under Chester Road at Tyburn House at the Kingsbury Road junction. On 3 March 1931 bus 58 (OF 3967) is parked opposite the Tyburn House public house on the 21 route; this service ran from that pub along Chester Road, Station Road and Perry Common Road to terminate at College Road, Perry Common, and had only been introduced on 19 November 1930. The Tyburn House hostelry was built by Ansell's Brewery in 1930 to replace a much older Georgian inn that stood alongside Chester Road. The new building, designed by Bateman & Bateman, was a single-storey structure faced with dressed stonework and with large mullioned windows. A few months later No 58 would be sent to back Guy Motors for rebuilding into a B32F normal-control single-decker. *Birmingham Central Reference Library*

59 (OF 3968)

Middle Cotteridge's Victorian shopping centre developed around the junction of Pershore Road and Watford Road near the Midland Railway's Kings Norton station. Behind the trees and bushes on the right is the Wesleyan Methodist Church, built of brick with stone facings and consecrated in 1901. The shop with the sunblinds pulled down is Faulkes' grocery shop, opposite which was the terminus of the Pershore Road 36 tram route. Standing outside the 1920s-built showrooms of Birmingham Gas Department in 1930 is bus 59 (OF 3968), still then a normal-control vehicle. It is working on the 18 route between Kings Norton Green and the Bell public house in Northfield, which had been introduced on 20 March 1929. The 18 was precisely the sort of suburban bus service that best suited these buses in their unrebuilt state. *B. Geens collection*

60 (OF 3969)

Bottom The last of the Guy 'Conquest' Cs of 1929, No 60 (OF 3969), by now rebuilt to a forward-control bus, stands

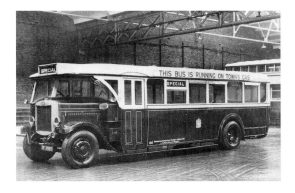

in Harborne Garage; in its reincarnation as a 32-seater, it was a much more useful bus and could be used on a much wider range of routes. In the days before diesel engines were fully developed, a number of experimental fuels were introduced around the country, including such oddities as creosote; No 60 was converted to operate on compressed town gas for the British Industries Fair of February 1933. These fairs were held annually in Chester Road as an international showcase for the products of Birmingham and the West Midlands, and a bus running on an experimental fuel system was too good an opportunity to miss, so the use of No 60 on the service to the Castle Bromwich site was not altogether surprising. It ran in this condition for exactly two years before being reconverted to run on petrol by the beginning of March 1935. After all this expense, it was withdrawn just two months later. *Author's collection*

338-367 (OF 3970-3999)
AEC 'Regent' 661; AEC A145 7.4-litre petrol engine; Brush H26/24R body; es 10.1929-1.1930, w 1.1930-12.1950

Nos 338 and 339 were the 10th and 11th of the 12 AEC 'Regent' prototypes (chassis numbers 661.010 and 011). They were the first double-deckers to be purchased with totally enclosed staircases and drivers' cabs and were the first that could be regarded as modern. They had just one step on to the platform, as the chassis was of a genuinely low height. They had 'piano-front'-style Brush bodies, which were to become the signature of all the AEC 'Regents' bought by Birmingham during this period. No 344 had the first BCT straight staircase, but this design was not repeated as it gave a full-width rear platform; 361-367 were fitted with Leyland diesel engines and torque converters in 1934-43; 359 ran on producer gas during the war; 359 and 362 were painted grey during the war; 341/2/3/5/7/50/2/8/9/62 rebodied Brush MoS H30/24R and 346/53/56 rebodied Brush MoS H30/21R 1943-44; 339 to driver trainer 56, 1938.

339 (OF 3976)
Below left No 339 (OF 3976) stands in the yard of the Brush factory in Loughborough in the first week of November 1929. This was the second of the two pre-production prototype chassis, which within six months would be returned to AEC and replaced by two new ones. These first two 'Regents' could be distinguished from subsequent deliveries as their radiators had slightly more curved header tanks. The sleek Brush 50-seat bodies were a revelation when compared to those on the ADC 507s, the last of which had been delivered only nine months earlier. Their low rear platform access, enclosed staircase and fully glazed driver's cab, as well as their powerful 7.4-litre petrol engine, gave the look of being right up-to-the-minute. The passengers were well provided for: the upholstered, cushioned seats, polished wood-lined window frames and bulkheads, plywood panelled ceilings, and smooth comfortable ride must have been a dramatic improvement over what had come before. *Brush, Loughborough*

341 (OF 3973)
Below The plan for an Outer Ring Road was defined by the City Surveyor in 1911, while the widening of Lordswood Road, which would be part of this grand design, was initially proposed under the UK's first Town Planning Act of 31 May 1913. This was intended to be the first stage in the opening up of the western edge of Harborne and the newly acquired farmland in Quinton for private and municipal housing, but work was suspended until about eight years after the end of the First World War. It was not until the end of the 1920s that the 100-foot-wide, tree-lined road with wide grass verges was completed, just after the new Outer Circle bus route was opened. Working on the 11 route, AEC 'Regent' 341 (OF 3973) passes Kelmscott Road, on the extreme right, travelling towards the Kings Head on 19 September 1935. The rear of these

Brush-bodied buses was very square and lacked both an emergency exit from the upper saloon and the later Board of Trade requirement of an 18-inch cut-away to the back platform that would also serve as an emergency exit to crawl through in the event of the bus turning over on to its nearside. *Birmingham Central Reference Library*

353 (OF 3985)

Top Pure suburbia! The road layout in Acocks Green village was remodelled in 1932, resulting in the 44 tram route's fourth terminus, this time in the middle of the traffic island. Standing alongside the substantial wooden passenger shelter is tram 142, waiting to return to the city. Alongside the New Inn public house, which had also re-opened in 1932, bus 353 OF 3985) of December 1929 is standing at the terminus of the 1A route before leaving for the city centre by way of Moseley Village and Five Ways. The 1A route had come into existence on 7 April 1926 when the 11 Outer Circle service had been introduced. The distant bus is a Vulcan-bodied AEC 'Regent', which is about to turn right into Dudley Park Road on the Outer Circle route. The section of the original 11 route between Moseley and Acocks Green had been abandoned, becoming an extension of the existing 1 route at this time. No 353 will turn sharp left into Wesley Road in front of the open space that, prior to 1931, had been the site of the original early-19th-century New Inn. The Municipal Library, just to the left of the new pub, was another 1932 newcomer, opening on 14 June. The 44 tram route would be converted to buses on 6 January 1937, but the 1A route would continue its circuitous journey to the city and still departs today from the same point. *Author's collection*

356 (OF 3988)

Above The bus routes to Kingstanding's large private and municipal housing estates were first opened in August 1930 when the 33 route was introduced to Ellerton Road by way of Newtown Row, Perry Barr and Kingstanding Road. This was the first time that a bus service, rather than a tram route, had become the main public transport provider to a newly developed suburb. Bus 356 (OF 3988) was one of the dozen 338-367 class of 661s rebodied by Brush with an MoS-style H30/21R body, in this case in September 1943. By 1949, because of their poor fuel economy and advancing years, these Birchfield Road Garage-based buses were being restricted to peak-hour extras and shortworkings. No 356 is heading towards Perry Barr on the 25 peak-hour service and is accelerating from the last section of dual-carriageway on the hill in Kingstanding Road at Crossway Lane. The 25 was a peak-time service that left the Finchley Road terminus shared with the 33 route to Kingstanding, and, on reaching Perry Barr, 'switched' routes and went via Villa Cross and Hockley into the city centre by way of the 29 route. To the right of the bus, the houses are privately owned late-1920s properties. *2489 Group collection*

357 (OF 3989)

At 12.55pm on a warm sunny day in August 1930, four AEC 'Regent' 661s stand in Paradise Street; such a day would be ideal for going to the races, and in those days Birmingham had a racecourse at Bromford Bridge, which survived until its last meeting on 21 June 1965. Behind the bus is the Birmingham & Midland Institute; designed by Edward Barry and opened after much delay in 1860, it was a pioneer of adult education classes in Britain – one wonders if they ever did classes in bookmaking for turf accountants! The leading bus is 357 (OF 3989), filling up with racegoers who would find the upper saloon more reminiscent of a gentlemen's club than a bus, while the lower saloon was more akin to a hotel sitting room. Another of the class stands behind it, but the second and third are two of the eight English Electric-bodied buses from the 369-407 batch of 'Regents' that entered service during August 1930. *G. H. F. Atkins*

61-80 (OF 6071-6090)
Guy 'Conquest' C; Guy 7.672-litre petrol engine; Guy B26F body; es 2.1930-3.1930, w 12.1934-1.1936

These were all rebuilt by being lengthened by the half bay behind the entrance and converted to forward-control and their seating capacity increased to B32F, between December 1931 and February 1932. For further details see 51-60 (page 49).

64 (OF 6074)

Speeding away from the 22 route terminus at the John Bright Street end of Station Street is single-decker OF 6074, passing a brand new parked Morgan F4 three-wheeler registered in December 1934. No 64 is in its lengthened forward-control condition, which was completed in February 1932. The Guy 'Conquest' Cs looked a lot more purposeful in this form, and were much more useful buses with their increased seating capacity, though they retained the armchair-like moquette-covered seats. Despite the expense of their dramatic conversion, most of the 30 'Conquests' only remained in service until the delivery of the Metro-Cammell-bodied AOP-registered Daimler COG5s in June 1935. This left just four of them in service, and these were replaced in January 1936 when the BOL-registered batch of new Daimler COG5s was delivered. *J. E. Cull*

74 (OF 6084)

Right The 'Conquest' was an imposing yet attractive-looking bus in its normal-control condition, although with its long bonnet it seemed to be more engine than bus! No 74 (OF 6084) was one of the batch of 20 that entered service in early 1930 and were identical to the 51-60 batch of the previous year. In August 1930 it is waiting at the city terminus of the 22 route in Station Street beneath the premises of furrier Sidney & Co on the corner of Hill Street, where the enclosed bogie tram is speeding past on its way to the 37 terminus; the following year Sidney's was taken over by another furrier called Marks. The 22 route to Bolton Road,

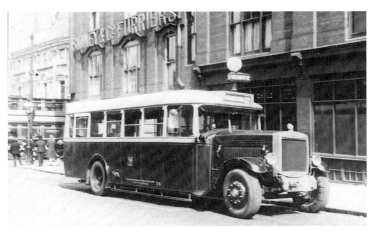

Small Heath, had been Birmingham's second tram service to be abandoned, on 5 February 1930; as the route served the BSA factory, the peak-hour workings to coincide with the factory whistle must have been very busy. Unfortunately, for the rest of the day the route was unprofitable, though after conversion the use of single-deckers with only 25 seats must have caused overloading problems at the start and finish of the factory's shifts. *G. H. F. Atkins*

75 (OF 6085)

Below Now this is the sort of work for which the 30 Guy 'Conquest' Cs were intended! The little boy on his 'fairy cycle' looks on as bus 75 (OF 6085) travels along the council-house-lined St Heliers Road, Northfield, having left the distant terminus in front of the houses at the end of the road. It is about to cross the Lockwood Road junction where the woman and her young daughter are walking. It is working on the 23 service between the introduction of the route on 30 July 1930 and the end of 1931, when it went back to Guy Motors to be rebuilt to forward control. The Tinkers Farm and Allen's Cross estates in Northfield were built on what had recently been farmland, and were completed in the last half of the 1920s; the original 18 bus route began operating into Allen's Cross on 2 February 1930, terminating in the distance at the end of St Heliers Road at Barnsdale Road. *B. Geens collection*

96 (OF 8368)
AEC 'Regent' 661; AEC A145 7.4-litre petrol engine; Short H28/24R body; b 1.1930, w 7.1944

This was originally an AEC demonstrator that entered service in January 1930 and was numbered 96 in the demonstration series. The Short metal-framed body seemed to have an even more exaggerated style of 'piano front' than normal, having three rear windows in each saloon. No 96 was purchased by BCT in March 1930 and was immediately re-numbered 368 in the main fleet number series. It was the first bus in the fleet to have a matching fleet and registration number.

96 (OF 8368)
Below The Short Brothers body on 96 was a 'one-off' design with some features common to Short lightweight tramcar 842, such as the window pan design and the raised waistrails below each saloon's windows. Like the tram, it was of all-metal construction and aluminium alloys were used for the upper saloon floor, frame and roof, although the lower saloon floor and platform were made of wood. It had

an ornate interior that at first sight looked similar to 842's, and the 'piano-front' design had a greater slope than any other AEC 'Regent' delivered between 1929 and 1932. The renumbered 368 (OF 8368) stands at the bus stop in Paradise Street in about 1932, working on the 1A service to Moseley and Acocks Green. To the left is Ratcliff Place and the Town Hall, while in the background, on the corner of Victoria Square and New Street, is Galloway's Corner. The bus still has the rather splendid large front sidelights as well as its primrose-painted bonnet top, which with only one exception was a feature that would not be repeated until the first 'New Look'-front bus, 2426, was delivered in February 1950. *R. Marshall*

96 (OF 8368)
Bottom The days when 96 was nicknamed 'The Showboat', because of its luxurious interior fittings, are long since gone as the bus, by now 368 (OF 8368), stands in Yardley Wood Garage on 15 September 1944, discarded with the disused producer gas trailers. The bus has white-painted edges to the platforms and looks as if it is about to go out for a day's work, but appearances are deceptive, as the destination boxes are without blinds. Although No 368's body shows very little sign of sagging or distortion, it has been out of use since its withdrawal from service at the end of July 1944. The unusual rear end featured three upper saloon windows, and a general similarity of design to the prototype lightweight tramcar 842. This view shows that it has a curved staircase, making it almost certainly the last Birmingham bus not to have a straight one. *L. W. Perkins*

96 (UK 8911)
Guy FCX66; Guy 7.672-litre petrol engine; Guy H27/26R body; b 6.1930

This was a six-wheeled vehicle that Guy Motors demonstrated from 14 June 1930 to 11 January 1932; it was operated from Harborne Garage where all the six-wheeled fleet were eventually housed. Despite its 18ft 6in wheelbase and length of nearly 30 feet, its Guy body had a seating capacity of only 53. Hall Lewis was rescued from bankruptcy and reformed as Park Royal Coachworks on 12 April 1930, but this does not look like a product of either companies.

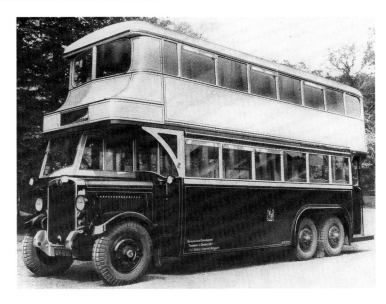

96 (UK 8911)
Again, recourse to an official Guy Motors photograph has to be made as there are no known picture of Guy FCX demonstrator 96 (UK 8911) in service. It was basically a six-wheeled version of the 'Invincible' model, and had an exaggerated style of 'piano front' between the cab and the front of the set-back upper saloon. This body was almost certainly built by Guy Motors itself as it looked virtually the same as that mounted on Guy BTX trolleybus demonstrators 18 (UK 8341) and 19 (OG 9886). Although 96 remained in the city for 19 months, running on the Outer Circle route, it did not generate any orders. *Guy Motors/R. Marshall collection*

– (JF 223)
AEC 'Regent' 661; AEC A145 7.4-litre petrol engine; Ransomes Simms & Jefferies H27/22R body; b ?.1930

This AEC, Southall, demonstrator was built for Leicester Corporation, and was demonstrated to Birmingham during July 1930.

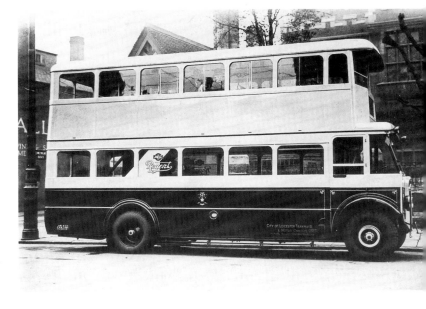

– (JF 223)
This is what JF 223 looked like when it was being demonstrated to Leicester City Transport on 1 June 1930. It had an LGOC-style Ransomes Simms & Jefferies 49-seat body and came to Birmingham in July 1930, where its new type of 110hp 7.4-litre petrol engine was available for Birmingham's engineers to test. It obviously wasn't a great success either in Birmingham or Leicester as it was quickly sold to G. F. Campion of Ruddington. *J. Cooper*

338-339 (OG 3638-3639)
AEC 'Regent' 661; AEC A145 7.4-litre petrol engine; Brush H27/21R body; es 8.1930; rebodied Brush H30/24R 1944; w 4.1938-12.1950

These two buses had new chassis supplied by AEC, which exchanged the two original prototypes that were the first buses numbered 338-339.

338 (OG 3638)

The replacement chassis for the original 338 was registered OG 3638 and went into service on 1 August 1930 with the 1929 body from its numerical predecessor. In January 1944 it re-entered service with an MoS-type Brush body. 'Birmingham buses completing their work' might be the title for this photograph as 338 stands rather sadly on the forecourt of Birchfield Road Garage on New Year's Eve 1950, having completed the last working of a petrol-engined bus in passenger service in the city as well as being the final AEC 'Regent' to operate in revenue service. The occasion was marked by the driver and two Birchfield Road mechanics posing for the camera before 338 was driven away for storage and subsequent scrapping at Bird's yard in Stratford. *Author's collection*

98 (VM 5621)
Vulcan 'Emperor' VWBD; Vulcan 'Monarch' petrol engine; Brush H27/21R body; b 10.1930

This Vulcan Motors demonstrator was used between 14 October 1930 and 8 January 1931. The 'Emperor' was not a very successful double-decker, with only Glasgow, Liverpool and Southport, where it was made, purchasing it in any quantity, although a BCT driving instructor once told the late Ray Coxon that it was 'the nicest bus he had ever driven'.

98 (VM 5621)

This is *probably* the vehicle demonstrated to Birmingham for two months at the end of 1930, although by the time it arrived it was painted in full BCT livery. This was the fifth Vulcan 'Emperor' VWBD to be built and was the second demonstrator, although originally it had a much smaller old-fashioned radiator. The body was built by Brush to a completely different design from those supplied earlier in the year. VM 5621 was offered to Glasgow Corporation in December 1931, which had bought 25 air-braked Cowieson-bodied 'Emperors'. *Author's collection*

369-407 (OG 369-407)
AEC 'Regent' 661;
AEC A145 7.4-litre petrol
engine; English Electric
H27/21R body; b 8-12.1930;
374/98 rebodied Brush
MoS H30/24R 1943; 369/77/
78/79/85/87/91/95/97/99/
401-3 rebodied Brush
MoS H30/21R 1943;
w 1.1938-12.1950

The composite English Electric bodies had a 'piano-front' style body. Nos 373/81/83/93 were painted grey during the war and 377/80/89/92/99 ran on producer gas; 388/414/416 to driver trainers 55/57/58, 1938.

378 (OG 378)

Above right From the 1920s until the late 1950s, extra destination information was carried on yellow-painted radiator slip-boards, one of which, apparently handwritten, showing 'Dudley Road', is being carried by 378 (OG 378). This AEC 'Regent' had been rebodied in August 1943 with an austere Brush H30/21R straight-staircase body that used the deep upholstered seats from other pre-war bodies they had replaced. It is turning from Winson Green Road into Dudley Road to terminate outside Summerfield Park, on a shortworking on the 11 service. By this stage of its career, it was operating out of Birchfield Road Garage, the last one to operate petrol-powered buses in Birmingham. Behind the bus is a little pre-war Bedford pick-up van, turning left into Dudley Road in front of Wickett's grocery shop, while parked outside Cox's bakery shop is a 1938 Austin Cambridge 10/4 saloon. *R. F. Mack*

388 (OG 388)

Right This evocative scene among the run-down 19th-century buildings in Snow Hill is not quite what it seems, as bus 388 (OG 388) travels up the hill towards the city centre. It is the summer of 1945, and although it has a wartime grey roof, it is not in passenger use, having been taken out of service in May 1938 to be used as a driver trainer until the autumn of 1947. It then received, uniquely, a Metro-Cammell metal-framed body from one of the 484 class, then within a year was rebodied again with a 'utility' Brush body. It is overtaking a mid-1930s Fordson B lorry and is being followed by an Austin 10/4 car, which could be a convertible or a cabriolet, dating from

about 1936. Travelling down the hill is Leyland 'Titan' TD6c 283 (EOG 283), on the 74 service to Dudley and still sporting its dark grey wartime camouflage-painted rear dome. This Metro-Cammell-bodied bus dated from April 1939 and came into service when the tram services to Handsworth and beyond were abandoned on 1 April of that year; the remains of the tram tracks can be seen in the cobbles in the foreground. The only building to survive today is the towered end of the red brick and terracotta Red Palace, on the corner of Constitution Hill and Hampton Street, dating from 1896 and dedicated to the memory of Lord Roberts of Kandahar. The distant church is Thomas Rickman's impressive Gothic revival church of St George's; built in 1820, it closed in 1950 and was pulled down ten years later. *Birmingham Central Reference Library*

392 (OG 392)

Below Kingstanding was part of Perry Barr UDC until 1928, and at that time contained just four farms on the exposed heathland that rose steeply to the north of the Tame valley. Just as when Quinton was taken over in 1909, Kingstanding was seen as an ideal site to build a new municipal housing estate to take people out of the squalor of the blighted back-to-back housing in the inner-city areas. Birmingham Council was quickly off the mark, and by 1932 some 6,300 houses had been built, providing homes for 30,000 people, whose demand for public transport led to the introduction of the 33 bus service. The last tram route extension had been opened to another similar municipal housing estate in Stechford on Tuesday 26 August 1928, so Kingstanding might have been served likewise, from the Perry Barr terminus of the 6 tram route. The Corporation had the Parliamentary powers to do this, so it was perhaps surprising that for the first time motorbuses were introduced, on 18 August 1930 to Ellerton Road. The 33 was extended to its second and longest-standing terminus at the Finchley Road/Kings Road junction in January 1933, and standing there on Saturday 31 July 1943 is 392 (OG 392), which had been converted to run on the inefficient producer gas system just one month earlier. *L. W. Perkins*

393 (OG 393)

Bottom Industrial Witton straddled the Tame valley, with Kynoch's Lion Ammunition Works occupying the north side of Brookvale Road and the GEC electric traction motor factory off Electric Avenue and Deykin Avenue to the east. Crossing the recently widened River Tame bridge in Brookvale Road is bus 393 (OG 393), coming towards Witton Square on 4 February 1937 on the 7 route to Portland Road. This route was introduced on 26 September 1927 as the southbound leg of the cross-city route from Perry Common; in the northbound direction it was numbered 5. Only four years earlier this bus had been used in somewhat abortive experiments using creosote as a fuel. *Birmingham Central Reference Library*

408 (OG 408)
AEC 'Regent' 0661; AEC A155 8.1-litre diesel engine; English Electric H26/21R body; es 4.1931, w 4.1938

This bus had a 'piano-front'-style body and was the first AEC bus to be delivered with a heavy oil (diesel) engine.

408 (OG 408)

The last of the 40 English Electric-bodied 'Regents', 408 (OG 408) was identical to the remainder except for being a genuine (ie not converted) 0661 model. Its upper seating capacity was reduced in order for it to pass the stringent tilt-test regulations and still have an unladen weight within the legal restrictions. It could easily be identified from the offside by having a slight 'snout' to allow for the extra length of the diesel engine. It is seen in Harborne Garage where many of the early diesel experiments took place. It was converted to petrol in October 1937 and withdrawn six months later. *Author's collection*

---

209 (OG 209)
AEC 'Regent' 661; AEC A145 7.4-litre petrol engine; MCCW H27/21R body; es 11.1930, w 9.1945

This was one of several prototype MCCW metal-framed bodies and was MCCW Contract No 2. It was the second metal-framed body to be purchased by Birmingham, but as usual had a 'piano-front'-style body.

209 (OG 209)

When new, 209 (OG 209) suffered the indignity of having a railway wagon shunted into its side to show off the structural integrity of the still new metal-framed body concept. Afterwards, 209 led a fairly uneventful life until withdrawal in September 1945, although it did run on producer gas during 1944 when allocated to Perry Barr Garage. Towards the end of its service life it was allocated to Yardley Wood Garage, and, looking a little battered, it stands outside the garage in Yardley Wood Road on Thursday 12 July 1945 as another driver poses with the regular crew before they go into Birmingham on a 24 route shortworking to Ethel Street. *L. W. Perkins*

95 (UK 7456)
Sunbeam 'Sikh' K101; Sunbeam 7.982-litre petrol engine; Dodson H35/32R body; b 7.1929

The six-wheeled 'Sikh' was an attempt by another failing car manufacturer to break into the bus and coach industry at the end of the 1920s. Only three 'Sikh' chassis were built, the first being converted to the prototype MS1 trolleybus, JW 526, while the third was not bodied until 1932, when it had a very brief life with Westminster, a London independent. The second chassis had a more varied career as the Wolverhampton company's demonstrator, and was used by Birmingham for just three weeks from 5 November to 1 December 1930. It was sold in 1933 to Derby Corporation as its 44.

95 (UK 7456)
The six-bay Dodson 67-seater body on the 'Sikh' chassis looks quite impressive as UK 7456 is demonstrated on Leicester Corporation's 11 service in May 1930. While in Birmingham for three weeks it clocked up exactly 4,200 miles. A recently discovered photograph sees it working into Queen Square, Wolverhampton, some time during 1930, but despite its operation in its home town, even that operator failed to be impressed. *J. Cooper*

409-443 (OG 409-443)
AEC 'Regent' 661; AEC A145 7.4-litre petrol engine; Vulcan H27/21R body; b 8.1930-11.1930; 418 rebodied Brush MoS H30/24R 1944; 412/29/35/38/40/43 rebodied Brush MoS H30/21R 1943; w 7.1937-11.1950

This was Vulcan's interpretation of the BCT 'piano-front'-style body, and they were the only Vulcan bodies ever built for Birmingham. Nos 420/21/25/34/35 were painted grey and 421/35 ran on producer gas during the war.

412 (OG 412)
Passing over the tram tracks coming out of Martineau Street recently vacated by tram 771 on its way to Washwood Heath on the 10 route, OG 412 is travelling along Corporation Street towards New Street on the 9 route to Quinton. This route was first operated on 31 March 1919 as far as the Stag & Three Horseshoes public house at the top of Mucklow Hill, then at some point it was curtailed to the city boundary. No 412 is passing beneath the upstairs offices of the Car & General Insurance Corporation and alongside the retail premises of Thomas Cook. This was before 5 June 1933, when the infamous anti-clockwise city-centre one-way system was introduced. The 1930 Midland Red SOS single-decker, on its way to Walsall, passes the impressive bus stop used by services 1A, 5, 6 and 29, suggesting that this picture was taken in the autumn of 1930. *Author's collection*

421 (OG 421)

Above Bus 421 (OG 421) stands at the Finchley Road terminus of the 33 route on 31 July 1943. It was painted grey in 1942 and converted to run on producer gas from June 1943 until its withdrawal at the end of June 1944. It is waiting with its anthracite-burning trailer for another wheezing and painfully slow journey to the City Centre. In 1942 the Ministry of War Transport issued instructions that 10% of motorbus fleets with a strength of more than 100 vehicles had to be converted to producer gas operation, and 421 was one of 25 petrol-engined 'Regents' to be treated. This Government attempt to conserve precious petrol supplies was not successful despite a huge capital investment at Perry Barr Garage, from where all the gas-powered buses operated. *L. W. Perkins*

440 (OG 440)

Below A paper sticker in the front window tells us that OG 440, formerly fitted with a Vulcan body, will shortly be on its way 'DIRECT TO VILLA PARK', with a stipulation that it unloads in Witton Lane. No 440 was one of 50 petrol-engined 661s built between 1929 and 1931 to be rebodied with Brush MoS bodies, in this case in August 1943; it had a straight staircase taken from one of the replaced bodies. This reduced the seating capacity from the wartime norm of 56 to an H30/21R seating layout. In 1948 it is waiting on the wrong side of Carrs Lane for a rush of Villa Park-bound fans, outside Carr Lane Congregational Church, where the Rev A. S. Herbert will preach on the following evening. *S. N. J. White*

94 (VR 9019)
Crossley 'Condor'; Crossley 6.8-litre petrol engine. Crossley L26/24R body; b ?.1930

This lowbridge 50-seater was a Crossley Motors demonstrator in Birmingham between 10 October 1930 and December 1931, and was operated from Barford Street Garage, running 33,572 miles in service. There is no known photograph of it.

100 (VC 7519)
Daimler CH6; Daimler 5.6-litre petrol engine; Buckingham H26/24R body; b 2.1931

This double-decker was a Daimler demonstrator from 6 March 1931 to 30 June 1934, and had one of the last bodies built by John Buckingham of Bradford Street, Birmingham, before that company fell victim to the Depression. It worked mainly from Perry Barr Garage, clocking up 84,491 miles and receiving an overhaul in April 1933. The success of the pre-selector gearbox and fluid flywheel led to the ordering of the Daimler CP6s of 1933.

100 (VC 7519)

Although VC 7519 was well travelled around the West Midlands, it was photographically very elusive. It started life as a demonstrator for one month as Walsall Corporation's 100, registered DH 8638. After leaving Birmingham it went to Coventry where, yet again, it was numbered 100, lasting until the body was burned out in 1938. This view of High Street, Coventry, in about 1936 shows the bus in the distance with a Coventry Corporation tramcar, 68, on the left. A slight 'piano-front' effect on the otherwise quite modern-looking Buckingham body can be just made out. The chassis later reverted to its original registration and was fitted with a full-front Holbrook single-decker body for use as transport for an all-ladies orchestra. *Commercial postcard*

93 (PL 3078)
Dennis 'Lance'; Dennis 6.13-litre petrol engine; ? H27/24R body; b ?.1931

This was the Guildford company's 'V'-fronted demonstrator from 7 March 1931 to 15 May 1931. Not much is known about it, to the extent that the body's origins are obscure, although it could have been a Park Royal product.

93 (PL 3078)

PL 3078 was only the fourth Dennis 'Lance' to be constructed and was tried out on the Inner Circle 8 route, running 3,423 miles in March 1931, after which it was not used again. It appears to be posed outside Barford Street Garage in front of the grim three-storey Victorian back-to-back courtyards that faced on to Barford Street; the garage was the first operational purpose-built one to be used by the Transport Department, having been converted from a factory and opened in June 1925. The bus had a fully-floating cab, the gap behind the driver's door being sealed with thick leather, as more usually found on contemporary single-deckers. *Author's collection*

92 (MV 489)
AEC 'Renown' 663; AEC A145 7.4-litre petrol engine; Brush H33/25R body; b 10.1931, w 7.1937

This was an AEC demonstrator from 23 October to December 1931, and was one of only three 'Renown' 663 three-axle chassis built for any operator (other than LGOC/LPTB) to be bodied and enter service; the other two went to Glasgow and Northampton Corporations. The Brush six-bay body had radiused saloon windows and was a 'piano-front' version of that built by the Loughborough-based coachbuilder on the AEC 663T trolleybuses 12-16 (OJ 1012-1016), which had entered service in September 1932. MV 489 was purchased in December 1931 as 92.

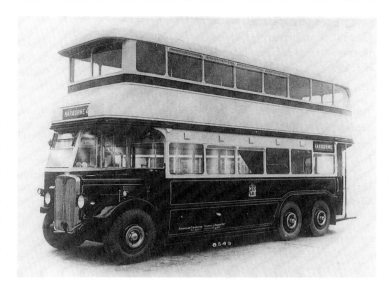

92 (MV 489)

Above right The massively impressive 92 (MV 489) was photographed by Brush's official photographer in October 1931, who has unfortunately air-brushed out any indication as to where the picture was taken. Regrettably, this is the only known picture of 92 taken during its 5½-year operational life as a bus. As the destination blind suggests, it was operated from Harborne Garage together with the ever dwindling numbers of six-wheeled motorbuses, and amassed some 178,605 miles trundling around the Outer Circle route. So how did it manage to miss so many photographers' lenses? *Author's collection*

92 (MV 489)

Below The solitary 'Renown' 663 had a very short life as a bus. In February 1938 it was equipped with the crane from Service Vehicle 15, the former Karrier DD6 bus OP 238, and was also given the same number in the auxiliary fleet, to become the Transport Department's main recovery vehicle. It was used in so many recoveries that it was given the nickname 'The Ambulance'. On 17 June 1948 bus 617 (AOG 617), a Daimler COG5 built in 1934, was taken to Holford Drive and used as a dedicated turn-over practice bus for the first time; amazingly it was repeatedly used in this capacity throughout most of the 1950s. On its first day, still with all its window glass intact, the mechanic on MV 489 is about to turn on its winch and haul the unfortunate double-decker back on to its wheels. MV 489's most famous usage was another five years away, as a stand-by shunter during the movement of the last tramcars coasting down Carrs Lane as they travelled across the city on their way for scrapping on the evenings of 3 and 4 July 1953. *Author's collection*

81-90 (OV 4081-4090)
Morris-Commercial 'Dictator' H; Morris-Commercial 7.698-litre petrol engine; MCCW B34F body (Contract 8); es 11.1931-12.1931, w 6.1942-12.1945

The Morris-Commercial 'Dictator' H single-decker model was built at the new factory in Adderley Park, Birmingham, and this batch of ten was purchased about the time that the Guy 'Conquest' Cs were going back to Guy Motors for conversion to forward control, causing a shortage of single-decker buses. The bodies were of up-to-the-moment Metro-Cammell metal-framed construction, and identical buses were supplied to Edinburgh Corporation. It was the comparative frailty of the Morris-Commercial petrol engine that put them in the 'Second Division', being mainly employed as peak-time extras after the delivery of the Daimler COG5s of 1935. Although camera-shy, nine of the ten nominally lasted into the autumn of 1945, albeit without much use. Nos 81-3 were painted grey during the war.

90 (OV 4090)
The coal-mining village of Hamstead, where the first mine opened in 1880, lay on the northern flood plain of the River Tame, and was divided up between Birmingham and West Bromwich in 1928 when the Urban District of Perry Barr was abolished. This left the village and the Rocky Lane area to be administered by Birmingham, while the coal mine in Hamstead Road came under West Bromwich. The original bus service to Browne's Green, Handsworth Wood, from the Ivy Bush on Hagley Road, was taken over from BMMO on 5 October 1914 and given the number 10. Renumbered 2 on 1 March 1916, it was extended down Hamstead Hill to the village on 1 February 1932. Here it met the two bus services operated by West Bromwich Corporation, the 6 from that town's centre by way of Great Barr, opened in 1926, and the 21 route to the colliery from Carter's Green, which predated the 'Village' service by some seven years. The only thing that identified Hamstead as a mining village was the aerial ropeway that carried a continuous line of spoil buckets from the mine to the nearby Hamstead Brickworks Quarry, which was being infilled with colliery waste, and these can be seen just above the gable end of the shop behind the bus. No 90 (OV 4090) was the last of the batch of ten to enter service in November 1931, and in August 1938 a little boy and his mother, who is carrying the lad's tennis racket, run past the conductor with his Bell Punch ticket machine and money satchel to board the bus. It is glinting in the bright summer sunshine at the 2 route terminus in Hamstead village just beyond the row of shops in Old Walsall Road, ready for the return journey to the Ivy Bush. *R. T. Coxon*

444-483 (OV 4444-4483)
AEC 'Regent' 661; AEC A145 7.4-litre petrol engine; Short H27/21R body; es 8.1931-11/1931; 463 rebodied Brush MoS H30/24R 1943; 446/48/51/52/59/62/64/ 69/70/74/77/83 rebodied Brush MoS H30/21R 1943; w 3.1944-12.1950

These 40 buses had 'piano-front' composite bodies built by Shorts, though the design was less flamboyant than that built on 368. These were the first buses to comply with the 1930 Road Traffic Act with regard to the statutory number of emergency exits. Nos 445/46/48/52/68-72/74/75/77/80/81/83 were loaned to London Transport in October/November 1940; 444/49/57/58/72/80 were painted grey and 444/47/53/56/59/ 63/69-71/75/77/80/81/83 ran on producer gas during the war.

464 (OV 4464)
Opposite top Above the parked 1949 vintage Bradford CA van with its little flat-twin-cylinder 1005cc engine and the Ford Prefect E93A 10hp saloon, the man cleaning the upper storey windows of The Lamp public house on the left looks decidedly precarious as he stands on the ledge above High Street, Bordesley, on 6 January 1950. The buildings lining the north side of the road were a mixture of early-19th-century and much later and more imposing Victorian premises such as The Lamp and Barclays Bank, which is the one by the telephone box. The older, distant buildings were wedged between the junction of Coventry Road and the former GWR's brick railway viaduct. Many years later some of these premises became The Doll's Club, Birmingham's first 'strip club', and, until someone found out, railway passengers at Bordesley station could see directly into the 'artistes' dressing rooms; one keen voyeur was repeatedly fined for pulling the communication cord on suburban

trains! Having received its Brush utility body during September 1943, some 12 years after entering service, OV 4464 rumbles over the derelict Stechford tram tracks and the cobbled road surface as it works into Birmingham on a Learner Duty Special. Above it are the trolleybus wires for the Coventry Road routes, which had just 18 months left to run. *Author's collection*

470 (OV 4470)

Middle Going home from work with his coat over his arm and his right hand firmly clamped on the stanchion pole, a passenger stands on the platform of 470 as it turns into Villa Road from Hamstead Road on Friday 16 June 1950. Dating from September 1931, 470 (OV 4470) was rebodied with an MoS Brush H30/21R body, re-entering service in December 1943. It is unusual to see one of these petrol-engined buses actually working on an all-day service, in this case the cross-city 29A route from Baldwins Lane, Hall Green, to the Pheasey Estate. On the right, passing in front of Francis Hallam's Dispensing Chemist shop, is tram 589, a 1920 Brush-bodied, formerly open-canopied car mounted on Brush Burnley bogies, working on the inter-suburban 5 tram route between Lozells and Gravelly Hill; surviving the closure of the 5 service in October 1950, it was later extensively damaged in an accident in August 1951 and withdrawn. Between the tram and the bus, in front of Preedy's tobacconist shop, is an early post-war Daimler CVD6, nominally working on the cross-city 29 route, but carrying a radiator slip-board reading 'BULL RING', which means that it will turn back once High Street has been reached. No 470 was eventually exported to the High Level Bus Company, Colombo, Ceylon. G. F. Douglas

475 (OV 4475)

Bottom Pulling a producer gas trailer while working in Finchley Road on the 33 route on 31 July 1943, 475's Short Brothers body sports a grey roof and rear dome and the regulation blackout markings, but still has its pre-war lined-out livery. OV 4475 is standing in Sidcup Road, just one stop and a stiff climb from the 33 route terminus. It was one of the 30 buses loaned to London Transport in November 1940, where that month it ran 2,256 miles. It was converted to run on producer gas at the end of January 1943, and when the use of the dreaded anthracite-burning trailers ended exactly one year later, it was withdrawn. *L. W. Perkins*

484-503 (OV 4484-4503)
AEC 'Regent' 661; AEC A136 6.1-litre
petrol engine; MCCW H27/21R body
(Contract 5); es 12.1931-1.1932,
w 4.1944-12.1947

These were the last buses to have a 'piano-front'-style body. Originally there were to be 15 with MCCW bodies and five with Buckingham bodies, but the latter firm closed and the entire batch was bodied by Metro-Cammell. They were the first BCT class to have metal-framed bodies and, unlike all the other AEC 'Regent' 661 classes, none were ever rebodied with wartime replacements, and were the last 'piano-front' buses to remain in service. Nos 484-90/92-94/96/97/99-501 were loaned to London Transport during October/November 1940; 484/87/500 were painted grey and 484/503 ran on producer gas during the war; and 502 was fitted with a Leyland diesel engine and torque converter as a H25/21R in 1934-43.

484 (OV 4484)

Entering service in December 1931, 484 (OV 4484), the first of the batch, stands in Perry Barr Garage yard in December 1942 after becoming one of the first buses in the fleet to be repainted in the wartime grey livery as well as acting as the prototype Corporation bus conversion to producer gas. An anthracite store was set up at the garage to supply the 25 petrol-engined 'Regent' conversions, with facilities to load the trailers and get the fires going so that a supply of gas was available once the bus had been started using its normal petrol supply. The 'Regents' were allocated to the 33 service to Kingstanding, which ironically was one of the least suitable routes in the city for gas operation because of its hilly nature. No 484 was fitted with a bulkhead-mounted header tank, which pumped the gas into the modified engine. The theory was fine, but in reality the engine's efficiency was cut by nearly half, resulting in a much reduced top speed and a tortoise-like climb of High Street, New Town and Kingstanding Road, unless the petrol tap was put back on again! On the left is 1201 (FOF 201), a four-year-old Daimler COG5 with a Metro-Cammell H30/24R body, its rear dome painted an all-over camouflaged dark grey. *BCT*

488 (OV 4488)

The Ridgeway, according to Birmingham's first historian, William Hutton, in 1762, was 'the grandest ancient road I had ever beheld'. The three-quarter-mile Ridgeway ran alongside the wall of the 103-acre Witton Cemetery, opened for its first interments on 27 May 1863. On 14 September 1933, almost new petrol-engined bus 488 (OV 4488)

speeds northwards towards College Road, showing the wrong destination number – it should be showing 'PERRY COMMON 5'. The open space on the right would soon form part of the Gipsy Lane-Brookvale Park Road municipal housing estate, constructed in the mid-1930s. *Birmingham Central Reference Library*

494 (OV 4494)

In this 1932 view of Corporation Street, the everyday bustle in the city's most important shopping street seems strangely muted; although there are many pedestrians, traffic consists of just two buses and a cyclist! The buildings in shadow on the left were built in the 1880s and stood between Cherry Street and Bull Street. They were known as Cobden Chambers and included the Cobden Hotel and the Great Western Arcade, the entrance to which is behind the Midland Red single-decker. The new seven-storey Lewis's department store, designed by G. de C. Frazer and completed in 1929, stands out like a beacon among the old Victorian buildings from Joseph Chamberlain's 'Parisian Boulevard' period of the city's redevelopment, with their 50-year covering of soot and grime. In the distance is the Methodist Central Hall with its impressive tower, dating from 1903 and designed by E. and J. A. Harper. Behind the woman in her stylish coat and cloche hat, almost new bus 494 (OV 4494) loads at the stop just short of Martineau Street, from where the tram tracks emerge. It is working on the cross-city 7 route to Portland Road, Edgbaston, a destination reinforced by the radiator slip-board. *J. Whybrow*

95 (KJ 2918)
Tilling-Stevens E60A6; Tilling-Stevens 6-cylinder 76bhp petrol engine; Short H28/21R body; b ?.1931

This demonstrator was built specifically for demonstration in Birmingham between 11 December 1931 and 30 January 1933, but on its return to TSM it was not used again. The prototype E60A6 chassis had a BCT 'piano-front'-style body by Short Brothers, whose Rochester body plant was quite near TSM's Maidstone headquarters.

95 (KJ 2918)

This attractive bus was registered KJ 2918 by Tilling-Stevens with Kent CC in 1931. The chassis was fitted with a virtually standard Shorts' Birmingham-specification body, although it did seat an extra passenger in the upper saloon; it looked very similar to the Crossley 'Condor' 442, while the low-mounted radiator and long windscreen were vaguely reminiscent of the AEC 'Regent' RT type and the post-war Crossley DD42 series. No 95 was operated on the Inner

Circle service from Barford Street Garage and was worked really hard, totalling 32,976 miles during its loan period without apparently having been off the road for repairs. *TSM Motor*

91 (OV 4848)
Morris-Commercial 'Imperial' HD;
Morris-Commercial 7.698-litre petrol
engine; Short H26/22R body; b 12.1931

This was the prototype Morris-Commercial 'Imperial' HD chassis demonstrated in Birmingham from 19 January 1932 to June 1936. Again, a Short Brothers metal-framed body was fitted, but this time the 'piano-front' style was modified by the raked angle of the front profile.

91 (OV 4848)
Photographs exist of OV 4848 when brand new, as here in the Short Brothers official photograph taken alongside the River Medway in Rochester, Kent, and immediately after its return to Morris Motors. Yet despite its four-year stay in Birmingham, at Perry Barr Garage, no pictures of it in service have ever come to light. The 'Imperial' was the Birmingham-based company's attempt to break into the heavy double-deck market, and its demonstration period with the Corporation was successful, leading to the purchase of a further 50 from the total of 83 built. *Author's collection*

96 (RG 1675)
Crossley 'Condor'; Crossley 6.8-litre
petrol engine with Crossley 'Effortless'
gearbox; Crossley H24/24R body; b 10.1930

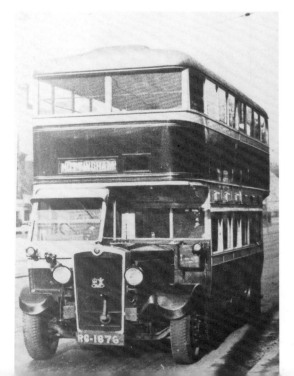

97 (RG 1676)
Crossley 'Condor'; Crossley 6.8-litre
petrol engine; Crossley H24/24R body;
b 11.1930

Both these were Crossley Motors, Manchester, demonstrators between 21 June and July 1932, having been registered by Aberdeen Corporation in November 1930. They had the standard Crossley six-bay bodies with a central raised roofline over the upper saloon gangway – Crossley's version of the Short 'camel roof' design, which gave the illusion of being low-height. Both buses stayed in Birmingham for only three weeks, to compare the different transmissions.

97, (RG 1676)
There is no known photograph of 96, or of either bus operating in Birmingham. No 97 (RG 1676), the second of the Crossley 'twins', was fitted with a normal crash gearbox, and after Birmingham it went back to Crossley Motors, where it was fitted with the Crossley VR6 9.12-litre high-revving direct-injection oil engine. The Autovac mounted on the lower saloon bulkhead was used to get the diesel from the fuel tank into the engine injectors. In this form it was demonstrated to Nottingham Corporation in 1932, and subsequently went to Northampton Corporation as No 66. It was rebodied with an East Lancs H30/24R body to a peacetime shape in 1944. *Author's collection*

442 (OJ 5442)
Crossley 'Condor'; Crossley VR6
9.12-litre diesel engine; Vulcan H27/21R
body; es 12.1932, w 12.1937

This was another Birmingham experiment with heavy oil, or diesel, fuel, which initially looked sufficiently promising for the Crossley chassis and engine to be purchased. No 442 had the Crossley VR6 indirect injection engine, which produced a good turn of speed and was a very smooth-running unit. However, compared to the petrol-engined equivalent, as with all early diesel engines, if it was not kept in tip-top order by the mechanical staff the bus could emit pungent black exhaust smoke. Chassis number 91057 was one of 100 buses in the 910 sanction of chassis to be fitted with the VR6 engine, which produced 100bhp at 1,700rpm. The Vulcan 'piano-front' body came from the previous AEC 'Regent' 442 (OG 442), which was used to replace the chassis of 424, whose chassis was returned to Southall in 1932.

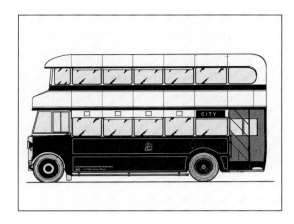

442 (OJ 5442)
There are no known photographs of this bus, the only pre-war Crossley actually purchased by the undertaking. This drawing gives a good idea of how 442 looked with its Autovac mounted on the bulkhead beneath the engine canopy. The Vulcan H27/21R body was modified to suit the Crossley 'Condor' chassis, and the bus was operated by Harborne Garage during its five years in service. *A. T. Condie*

93 (AHX 63)
AEC 'Q' 761; AEC A169
7.4-litre petrol engine;
MCCW H33/29F body
(Contract 23); b 10.1932,
w.10/1940

This was the first double-decker AEC 'Q' to be constructed, chassis number 761001. It was a revolutionary design with a front entrance, a set-back front axle and an offside-mounted engine between the axles outside the main chassis frame. Registered in Middlesex in December 1932, some two months after completion, AHX 63 was an AEC demonstrator in Birmingham from 28 January 1933 to 30 January 1934. It was

converted to 0761 with an A170 7.58-litre diesel engine during 1934 and came back to the city on 12 January 1935, having been away for nearly 12 months. It was painted in a reversed blue BCT livery, and was purchased by the Corporation on 16 October 1935 and reseated to H29/27F in 1936. It was well used for an experimental bus, covering 110,216 miles.

93 (AHX 63)
The revolutionary No 93 (AHX 63) waits to load up with passengers in Congreve Street, working on the 1A route to Acocks Green via Moseley Village. It was always painted in a reversed dark blue and primrose livery, although it's strikingly different appearance hardly needed this unique livery to make it stand out from the rest of the fleet. The front-entrance body was built by Metro-Cammell, though the design was influenced by AEC's Chief Designer G. J. Rackham, as well as showing the influence of the designers at LT's Chiswick Works. The body introduced the 'beaded' waistline, which produced a more balanced effect, especially beneath the lower saloon windows, and became a feature of all BCT buses from No 594 of 1934 until the last of the post-war 'standards' of October 1954. The main problem with the AEC 'Q' chassis was that because of the 26-foot-long Construction and Use Regulations, the rear overhang was of necessity pitifully short, and despite the use of very large single rear tyres, the bus was always a bit of a handful to drive in the wet, making it unpopular in those conditions. It always operated from Acocks Green Garage. *Author's collection*

93 (AHX 63)

It was barely four years since Birmingham had purchased the last of the outside-staircase ADC 507s, so the prototype AEC 'Q' must have been revolutionary for drivers, conductors and passengers. One can imagine how passengers who had just got used to the AEC 'Regent' buses with enclosed rear staircases, one of which is coming out of Broad Street, might try to get on at the back of 93, when both the entrance and the staircase were at the front. In tree-lined Calthorpe Road, Five Ways, in 1934, passengers are queuing to board the bus, working on the 1A route to Moseley and Acocks Green. In the background are the Victorian shops that stood between King Edward's Grammar School and Ladywood Road. *Author's collection*

---

94 (TF 7310)
Leyland 'Titan' TD2c; Leyland 7.6-litre petrol engine with torque converter gearbox; Leyland L24/24R body; b 5.1932

This Leyland Motors demonstrator was on loan to Birmingham from 16 February 1933 to 31 May 1934 to try out the new torque converter gearbox that was about to be fitted to AEC 'Regents' 361-367 and 503 in May 1934, coupled to either AEC or Leyland diesel engines.

94 (TF 7310)

The standard Leyland lowbridge body rather masks the importance of this TD2 demonstrator as it stands in the Leyland distributor's premises in Birmingham alongside the Leyland 'Tigress' normal-control coach in 1933. TF 7310 was used to test the Lysholm Smith torque converter gearbox, which was about to become the Leyland alternative to a crash gearbox. It was operated from Barford Street Garage and, with its lowbridge body, was used on the Inner Circle 8 route, where it amassed a total of 49,204 miles. The success of this type of gearbox led to further trials with five Leyland 'Titan' TD4cs in 1937 and the purchase in 1939 of the 135 TD6cs, built especially for the Corporation. TF 7310 was sold to James of Ammanford as that operator's 145. *Author's collection*

– (KV 1396)
Daimler COG5; Gardner 5LW 7.0-litre engine; Brush H28/26R body; b 7.1932

This was the Coventry firm's demonstrator and was on loan between 27 November and 15 December 1933. It was the first COG5 chassis to be constructed.

– (KV 1396)

If the Buckingham-bodied Daimler CH6, VC 7519, had an influence on the thinking of A. C. Baker and the Transport Committee, the demonstration of this bus, coming just a matter of weeks before the conversion of the Coventry Road tram route using

50 'state of the art' Leyland TTBD2 trolleybuses, made alternative ideas for future vehicles redundant overnight! Although the Brush bodywork was to a style purchased by Leicester City Transport and was therefore not up to Birmingham standards, the combination of the Gardner diesel engine and the pre-selector gearbox was irresistible and this bus presaged the purchase of more than 800 COG5s from Daimler. KV 1396 stands in the yard of the Brush body works in Loughborough when new in 1932. *Brush, Loughborough*

47-50 (OJ 9347-9350)
Morris-Commercial 'Dictator' H; Morris-Commercial 7.698-litre petrol engine; MCCW B34F body (Contract 30); es 5.1933, w 5.1945-12.1945

These were a further four locally produced Morris-Commercial 'Dictator' H chassis with metal-framed Metro-Cammell B34F bodies. Their front profile was altered with the front destination box being lowered to become part of the front dome. They were renumbered 77-80 in June 1935.

48, 49, 50 (OJ 9348/9/50)

Even more camera-shy than the batch purchased in 1931, three of the four 'Dictators' stand awaiting delivery at Metro-Cammell's Saltley Works in May 1933. The lower front destination box position gives the buses a more modern appearance, as does the deeper windscreen and the slight down-curve in the cab side windows. The buses were only in service for two years before they were superseded as front-line buses by Daimler COG5s, although they were kept busy working from Acocks Green Garage until after the outbreak of war. *Author's collection*

504 (OC 504)
Morris-Commercial 'Imperial' HD; Morris-Commercial 7.698-litre petrol engine; Brush H29/22R body; es 2.1934; reseated to H30/24R 1935

This was the first of just three Morris-Commercial 'Imperial' HDs to enter service, though it was two months after the last of the 47 Metro-Cammell-bodied buses. The attractive Brush body had a trace of the earlier 'piano-front' styling and it was the last bus to have the windows set deeply into the framework. Brush put a lot of effort into this metal-framed bus body in the attempt to gain a substantial order from Birmingham, with even the surrounds to the front destination box being chromed.

504 (OC 504)
On April Fools Day 1939 OC 504, numerically the first of the 'Imperial' double-deckers, waits at Six Ways, Erdington, working a Villa Park Football Special. The bus was operated from Perry Barr Garage, so this excursion around north Birmingham would not prove too strenuous for the frail petrol engine. It is parked outside the Erdington Branch of the Birmingham Municipal Bank on Gravelly Hill North, opened in the 1920s. No 504 would become the longest lived of the three 'odd'-bodied 'Imperials', being taken out of service at the end of April 1942, suggesting that major mechanical repairs were required at a time when Birmingham, like many other operators, was suffering a chronic shortage of buses. *L. W. Perkins*

505 (OC 505)
Morris-Commercial 'Imperial' HD; Morris-Commercial 7.698-litre petrol engine; English Electric H25/22R body; es 3.1934; reseated to H29/22R 1935; w 3.1941

English Electric, the company formerly known as the tramcar body builder United Electric Car Co, seemed to be willing to take orders for the production of small numbers of buses and coaches, although it was still the main suppliers of bodies to Ribble MS and some Lancashire municipalities. When new, the metal-framed body on 505 had only a seating capacity for 47 passengers.

505 (OC 505)
The bus waiting in the West Works of the English Electric Company factory in Preston prior to delivery to Birmingham is OC 505. English Electric appears to have dusted down the BCT body drawings for the AEC 'Regents' 369-408 of 1930, and put an almost straight raking front on the body, suggesting perhaps how much better the 'Regents' would have looked without the 'piano-front' body. The bus is equipped with four sets of Perry Barr Garage's destination blinds, where it spent its entire career in Birmingham. *J. H. Taylforth collection*

506 (OC 506)
Morris-Commercial 'Imperial' HD;
Morris-Commercial 7.698-litre petrol
engine; Gloucester RCW H26/22R body;
es 5.1934; reseated to H30/24R 1935;
w 6.1939

This was one of only a handful of double-decker chassis bodied by the Gloucester Railway, Carriage & Wagon Company. Surprisingly, in view of the excellent reputation of the company's railway carriages and wagons, its bus bodies were not very durable, so this unique metal-frame-body double-decker was not longed lived, even for a Morris-Commercial 'Imperial'.

506 (OC 506)
Bus 506 (OC 506) pulls away from the Beauchamp Avenue bus stop halfway down the steep Hamstead Hill on 13 August 1938. Although seemingly in good condition, it would be taken out of service at the end of the following June and stored for the duration of the Second World War; even then it was not until October 1946 that it was sold to Deveys, the Shenstone-based scrap merchant. This gives this bus the unenviable record of spending more than half of its 12-year life in storage. What a waste! The Perry Barr Garage-based Morris-Commercial is working on the cross-city 16A route, which was extended from Friary Road to Beauchamp Avenue on 27 October 1937, and will reverse into Beauchamp Avenue before returning across the city to Church Road, Yardley, as a 15, to which route it had been linked since 5 June 1929. In Birmingham, cross-city bus services were given a different number for each direction. *R. T. Coxon*

507-553 (OC 507-553)
Morris-Commercial 'Imperial' HD; Morris-Commercial 7.698-litre petrol engine; MCCW H28/22R body (Contract 35); es 9.1933-11.1933; reseated to H30/24R 1935; w.6/1939-6/1947

This class of 47 buses was the largest single batch of 'Imperials' to be constructed, and its intermediate design of bodywork was only produced for BCT on the Guy 'Arab' 208, the 17-66 batch of Leyland TTBD2 trolleybuses, and these buses. While the design was to have a great influence on all future Birmingham half-cab orders, the chassis was not very robust. Although the 7.698-litre petrol engine could propel the bus with a good turn of speed, it tended to have a short crankcase life, requiring constant retuning, had an extremely short brake-pad life, and a very awkward gearbox. The buses also gave a painfully rough ride. However, the engine and gearbox had the advantage of being mounted on a sub-frame that could be wheeled out quickly on the front axle, a useful feature given the regularity that the buses required repairs. Many of these buses were placed in store at the beginning of the war but 35 lasted until at least 1945.

509 (OC 509)
Below Six-month old bus 509 (OC 509) stands at the almost rural terminus at the junction between Alcester Road South and Druids Lane on Thursday 16 March 1934. Alongside it is the City of Birmingham boundary sign and a substantial wooden shelter of the sort still then being built for tram termini. A supposed maypole in the shape of a 40-foot-high inverted sword was used as a marker post at this important junction on the former turnpike road from Alcester, and stood in the left foreground; when May Day activities were

briefly introduced in the late 19th century, the name 'Maypole' was adopted. Gradually suburbia crept out from 'The Knob' at Alcester Lanes End to engulf the land up to the Solihull boundary on the north side of Maypole Lane, the large Maypole public house being one of the first buildings to open, on 17 July 1936. The bus is working back to the city on the cross-city 17 service to Chester Road, Erdington, introduced on 19 March 1928 and modified in August 1936, when the return journey was given the separate number 35. It was a semi-express service operating over the Moseley Road and Erdington tram routes and had a protected fares system, with fewer stops but at more cost to the passenger. As the Alcester Lanes End tram service was not extended, the service to the Maypole was a godsend for the Maypole community. The cross-city section of the route was curtailed on the outbreak of war, but the 35 continued as far as the City Centre until 1 October 1949 when the new tram replacement 48 and 50 routes used the Maypole as their new terminus. *Birmingham Central Reference Library*

517 (OC 517)
Opposite top The policeman on point duty in his white summer uniform appears to be distracted by something in John Bright Street as fairly well filled bus OC 517 storms up Hill Street, having come into the city from Church Road, South Yardley, on this hot summer's day in 1935. The metal-framed MCCW-bodied 'Imperials', with their highly polished chrome radiators, looked very up to date, although their Morris-Commercial 7.7 ohv petrol engines tended to backfire unless perfectly tuned. When, in the following year, Birmingham put out tenders for oil-engined chassis, it is said that a suitable design was being prepared in the drawing office at Adderley Park to be fitted with a Gardner 5LW unit, and Sir William Morris was so apoplectic that he stopped all further work on any of the large PSV designs and

almost immediately stopped production, leading to Charles Edwards, his Chief Engineer, leaving for Guy Motors. It could be argued that this period of body design was the best looking of all the pre-war 'Birmingham-style' bodies, being unencumbered by the thick upper saloon corner pillars introduced on the next class of BRCW-bodied Daimler CP6s. No 517 is passing the entrance to Queen's Drive, a private carriageway between the former LNWR and newer Midland Railway sides of New Street station. It is working on the cross-city 16 service, which had combined with the 15 to South Yardley in June 1929. *Author's collection*

523 (OC 523)

Middle On 3 July 1937 it is staff outing day at the Halford Works of Henry Hope & Sons, in Smethwick, and surprisingly not only had they hired three Birmingham Corporation double-deckers rather than coaches, but they had also been allocated three 'Imperials'; despite their well-made metal-framed bodies, they were notoriously poor-riding vehicles as their chassis were too light, inducing a very bouncy ride. One saving grace was that they were fast, which is perhaps why Acocks Green Garage used them. Here, 523 stands behind 551 (OC 551), and it is interesting that human nature hasn't changed as it is the top deck on both buses that is filling up rapidly. *H. F. Wheeler*

530 (OC 530)

Bottom In 1935 the Barrows Lane terminus of the 15A service was just beyond The Grange in Church Road, which from 1933 to 1989 was a Carmelite convent, and within hailing distance of the Ring o' Bells public house, then an Allsopp's hostelry housed in a double-bay-windowed house dating from 1860. Within little more than half a mile the bus would reach the Yew Tree junction at Stoney Lane on the Outer Circle route. OC 530, barely two years old, and with its seating capacity recently increased by four to 54, stands in the tree-lined road waiting for passengers, and for its conductor to change the destination blind to show 'Handsworth Wood 16' for the return journey. This was as close as Corporation buses ever got to the old village centre of Yardley, with its 13th-century church in the city's first Outstanding Conservation Area, finally recognised in 1976. *F. Lloyd*

554-563 (OC 554-563)
Daimler CP6; Daimler 6.56-litre petrol engine; BRCW H29/22R body; b 12.1933-1.1934; reseated to H30/24R 1935; w 1.1942-7.1945

These were ordered after the favourable impression made by VC 7519, and were the last petrol-engined buses to be delivered. They introduced the fluid flywheel and Wilson pre-selector gearbox into the fleet, and were the first batch of bodies built for the Corporation by the Birmingham Railway Carriage & Wagon Company of Smethwick. In all, 245 BRCW bodies were delivered to the undertaking between 1934 and 1940, when bus body production ended, giving the undertaking an alternative local supplier of bodies.

555 (OC 555)
The second terminus of the 16 route, established in October 1937, was in Beauchamp Avenue off Hamstead Hill, which had been developed as part of the Handsworth Wood Estate in 1934 and was the furthest north that this extensive housing development got, as further down Hamstead Hill was the wide flood-plain of the River Tame. At the terminus buses reversed into Beauchamp Avenue, with its small row of shops and Bundy Clock, against which the conductor at the back of OC 555 is leaning. The ten CP6s were allocated to Perry Barr Garage, where they ran alongside the Morris-Commercial 'Imperials', but the Daimlers were far more popular because of their fluid flywheels and Wilson pre-selector gearboxes, which made driving in the city's traffic much easier. Despite the destination display, the bus is actually working on the 15A route. *R. T. Coxon*

208 (OC 8208)
Guy 'Arab' FD; Gardner 6LW 8.4-litre engine; MCCW H29/22R body (Contract 41); es 5.1934; reseated to H30/24R 1935; w 2.1945

This and all subsequent buses were fitted with diesel (heavy oil) engines. BCT records state that 208 was rebuilt from Guy 'Invincible' FC 97 (UK 8047), though further investigation reveals that it might only have inherited its Gardner 6LW

engine. The Metro-Cammell bodywork was to the BCT 'interim' design, as on the Morris-Commercial 'Imperials' 507-553. Bus 208 was the last in the fleet to have a two-letter registration mark.

208 (OC 8208)
Aston Villa's latest football match has just finished, and all around the traffic island in Witton Square in 1935 are Football Special buses, including, outside the Co-Op, an ADC 507 with an outside staircase Shorts' body. Two very different

AECs are coming out of Witton Road on the right, an outside staircase 507 model and 494 (OV 4494), an MCCW-bodied 'Regent' built in 1931. The bus in the foreground, on an Outer Circle shortworking to Harborne, is 208 (OC 8208), and looks as if it has just escaped the approaching swarm of fans, much to the relief of the crew! Looking at first glance like one of the MCCW-bodied 'Imperials', this wide-radiatored double-decker was Birmingham's solitary pre-war Guy 'Arab' FD. Like all 'Arabs' it was fitted with an oil engine, in this case the usual Gardner 6LW 8.4-litre unit. Surprisingly, no more were purchased, and the Gardner-5LW-engined Daimler COG5 reigned supreme in the city's bus fleet. *Author's collection*

4.
1934-1938
DIESELS, STANDARDISATION, AND TRAM REPLACEMENT

The decision to order oil-engined buses from Daimler was a fairly momentous one in that it marked the beginning of a period of decision-making about what was to replace the tram routes as they came due for renewal. It is a myth that Birmingham Corporation Tramways & Omnibus Department was about to close down its tramway system after the closure of Nechells, Bolton Road and Hagley Road tram routes.

When the decision was made to close the Coventry Road tram routes and replace them with trolleybuses at a cost of £90,246 on 5 January 1934 it was done for purely pragmatic reasons. A new fleet of 50 Leyland TTBD2 six-wheeled trolleybuses with Metro-Cammell metal-framed bodies was purchased for the opening of the service and in 1937 a further 12 trolleybuses were bought, only this time they were four-wheeled Leyland TB5s.

It was only during 1936, when parts of the track on the Stratford Road tram routes became urgently in need of renewal, that the Council announced that after much deliberation that 'it would be in the best interests of the travelling public to abandon certain tramways as the tracks fall for renewal and to substitute some other form of vehicle and so gradually dispose of the tramcars.' This was in response to a local transport activist called Voigts who was pressurising the Transport Committee to adopt trolleybuses on the Stratford and Warwick Roads. The inner parts of the three Stratford Road routes were in dire need of replacement at an estimated cost of £120,000, and although the service had seen the penultimate track extensions from Highfield Road to the city

boundary at Shirley on 2 April 1928, they were very quickly suffering badly at the hands of the Corporation's own bus routes that had been developed in the late 1920s and 1930s, which were taking away trade from the main line services to Hall Green, Acocks Green and Stoney Lane, despite having a protected tram fare structure.

The trolleybus, despite being highly successful, especially on the recently converted Coventry Road route, was considered to be just as route-bound as the tramcar. The demonstration of the new Daimler COG5 bus with a pre-selector gearbox coupled to a 7-litre Gardner 5LW oil engine offered easy driving and a fuel consumption that was considerably more than three times more economical than a comparable petrol engine. By the end of 1934 the Daimler chassis had become Birmingham's preferred bus. Between 1934 and 1938 no fewer than 45 Daimler COG5 single-deckers and 665 COG5 double-deckers had been placed into service by the undertaking, while 19 new bus services were introduced during this period.

By the time that the two 1939 Dudley abandonments were imminent, such were the numbers of new buses required that Birmingham decided to dual source its future orders. This decision was based on the experiments made during 1937 when five AEC 'Regent' 0661s and five Leyland 'Titan' TD4cs were compared. The surprise was that the Leylands, with their fuel-thirsty Lysholm-Smith torque converter gearboxes, were ordered in preference to the 'Regents', which had the well-tried and fuel-efficient pre-selector gearboxes.

564-578 (AOB 564-578)
Daimler COG5; Gardner 5LW 7.0-litre engine; BRCW H26/22R body; es 5.1934-6.1934, reseated to H30/24R 1935; 11 of the class swapped bodies 1942-47; w 6.1946-12.1948

This was the first class of bus to combine the Gardner 5LW oil engine with the fluid-flywheel and Wilson pre-selector gearbox. The 5LW had a swept volume of 7.0 litres and gave an output of 85bhp at the governed speed of 1700rpm, which, combined with the fluid flywheel and pre-selector gearbox, produced a reliable, economical and, most importantly, easy to drive bus, to the point of being *almost* fool-proof. The bodies were built in Smethwick by BRCW and were very similar to those on the previous batch of Daimler CP6s.

567 (AOB 567)
Below Travelling out of the city along Hagley Road West in 1948 is bus 567 (AOB 567), working on the 9 route to the Birmingham boundary at Quinton. Originally this service went to the Stag & Three Horseshoes and the nearby little coffee house at the top of Mucklow Hill at Kent Road, but as this was outside the city boundary it had been taken over by Midland Red as part of its services to Halesowen and beyond. The 34 bus service as far as the Kings Head was introduced when the Hagley Road tram service was abandoned on 10 August 1930, and was twice extended to serve the new housing developments in the area, finally reaching just beyond the old tollgate in Hagley Road West on 18 February 1935 via a triangle using College Road and Ridgacre Lane. The bus has just left the Kings Head junction at Lordswood Road, and is passing the trees that lined Lightswood Park. It is overtaking KHA 431, a Morris-Commercial LC 30hp tilt van numbered 155 in the Midland Red service fleet. *R. G. Grosvenor via A. N. Porter*

569 (AOB 569)
Bottom Running past the grimy rusticated stonework of the colonnades in the podium of Birmingham Town Hall is a young schoolboy who appears to have just got off the less than two-year-old AOB 569, working on the 6 route into the city; this route was introduced on 29 September 1926 to the Bearwood boundary at the junction of Sandon Road and Willow Avenue, almost within sight of the Bear Inn junction at Three Shires Oak Road. No 569 is at the illuminated bus stop on the corner of Ratcliff Place (named after Sir John Ratcliff, Mayor of Birmingham 1856-59) and Paradise Street in the early months of 1936. Between the introduction of Birmingham's first one-way traffic scheme on 5 June 1933 and the revised second scheme of 17 August 1936, traffic coming from Broad Street was still able to access the City Centre Loop of New Street, Corporation Street, Bull Street and Colmore Row by travelling into Victoria Square by way of Paradise Street. Within two years 569 would be coming into the city by way of Edmund Street, at the other end of the Town Hall. Following the bus is a Morris-Commercial C type van dating from early 1934. *Author's collection*

579-593 (AOB 579-593)
Daimler COG5; Gardner 5LW 7.0-litre engine; MCCW H26/22R body (Contract 53); es 6.1934; reseated to H30/24R 1935; two of the class swapped bodies 1945; w 1.1946-12.1948

The Metro-Cammell bodies were different from the 1933 deliveries of Saltley-built bodies on the Morris-Commercial 'Imperial' double-deckers, having thick corner pillars at the front of the upper saloon. These were the last bodies to be delivered without a cream waistrail.

592 (AOB 592)
Above right All the vehicles travelling along Paradise Street on Monday 8 May 1944 will still have to wear the regulation blackout headlight masks for another six months, despite the last air-raid on Birmingham having been on 23 April 1943, when the final bombs fell on Drummond Road, Little Bromwich. In all, Birmingham received 77 air attacks, so it was little surprise that the city had a careworn look. The pre-war cream roofs on the buses had long since disappeared under camouflage grey paint. AOB 592, as with all the early classes of Gardner oil-engined buses up to bus 691, is fitted with an Autovac box on the bulkhead just below the front lower saloon window, whereas the later bus on the right, 932 (COH 932), a 1937 Metro-Cammell-bodied bus, has a well-hidden fuel pump instead. No 932 is working on the 9 route along Hagley Road West, while 592 is on the 10 service to Quinton Road West's municipal housing estate, started in 1939 but suspended in the spring of 1940 for the duration of the war. Between the two buses is a large Austin 20hp, while on the left is a 1939 Rover 16. No 592 is passing the imposing bulk of the Town Hall, outside which 569 stood nine years earlier. In the background is the impressive Flemish-Renaissance Christ Church Buildings, opened in 1900 to replace the 'wedding cake' Christ Church of 1813, which was pulled down in 1899 because of an infestation of death watch beetles. Known as Galloway's Corner, this curved block of shops and offices on the corner of New Street and Colmore Row survived the war and was demolished in 1970. *Birmingham City Transport/Kithead Trust*

593 (AOB 593)
Above Working on the 3 route on 10 May 1935, AOB 593 is the only motorised vehicle in Court Oak Road as it overtakes a two-wheeled horse and cart. The 3 route was extended from Queens Park to West Boulevard on 24 September 1930, where it turned at the future site of the Punch Bowl public house. It is passing Queens Park, opened to celebrate Queen Victoria's Golden Jubilee, as it approaches Hampton Court Road, and is in its original condition, with the number plate at the bottom of the radiator and the cab dash painted blue. It also has the Corporation's patented double-bladed, chain-driven horizontal windscreen wipers, which were on all deliveries of buses between 1929 and early 1936. *Birmingham Central Reference Library*

594-633 (AOG 594-633)
Daimler COG5; Gardner 5LW 7.0-litre engine; MCCW H26/22R body (Contract 68); es 11.1934-1.1935; reseated to H30/24R 1935; 20 of the class swapped bodies 1944-45; w 10.1947-3.1949

These Metro-Cammell bodies were of a new design, which, with only minor alterations, would remain the standard Birmingham style of straight-staircase bus body until the last Daimler COG5s were delivered in 1940. The general outline was softened and they were the first to have the cream waistrail below the lower saloon windows, a feature first seen on the AEC 'Q'. The driver's windscreen was at an angle when compared to the rest of the bus, in order to reduce any reflection from the lower saloon interior lights. No 596 was exhibited at the 1934 Commercial Motor Show (CMS).

623 (AOG 623)
Below Standing in Chapel Lane, Selly Oak, on 4 August 1940, AOG 623 is working on one of the many variations of the 20 service into the Weoley Castle estate. It is standing just short of the Plough & Harrow public house on the corner of Bristol Road, while in the foreground are the tram tracks used for depot workings to and from Selly Oak. No 623 has been recently repainted in the normal fleet livery, with a very artistic line in roof camouflage painting. While tramcars normally carried advertisements, buses generally did not until new contracts were signed in 1953 to regain the lost advertising revenue after the last tram abandonments. However, during the war they carried Government Public Announcement advertisements such as the one seen here, which were more proclamations than genuine advertisements and were usually to do with the financing of the war effort. *R. T. Wilson*

630 (AOG 630)
Bottom Bus 630 (AOG 630) entered service on New Year's Day 1935, and in June 1948 is standing outside the row of shops at the terminus of the 10 route in Quinton Road West, just beyond the Monarch public house. In the background are the late-1930s council houses, and a Fordson E83W van parked by a telephone box – why is a policeman skulking behind it? Opposite the pub and overlooking the Woodgate Valley was Tom Knocker's Wood, a fragment of woodland intended to be kept as an amenity for the new estate. However, during the early years of the war it became a hidden anti-aircraft gun battery site; alas, when fired the ack-ack guns blew down the very trees that were supposed to hide them, and that was the end of Tom Knocker's Wood! The bus's 12-year-old metal-framed body looks in quite good condition despite its imminent withdrawal within days of this photograph being taken! *E. Chitham*

634-673 (AOG 634-673)

Daimler COG5; Gardner 5LW 7.0-litre engine; BRCW H26/22R; es 12.1934-2.1935; reseated to H30/24R 1935; 10 of the class swapped bodies 1942-45; w 1.1946-11.1948

These 40 COG5s were the Birmingham Railway Carriage & Wagon Company's version of the Birmingham specification, and could be distinguished from the previous MCCW-bodied 593-633 class by having thicker upper saloon corner pillars and a thicker canopy panel over the rear platform.

641 (AOG 641)

Right New Street is arguably Birmingham's main shopping street, and although today it is a pedestrian precinct, many of the buildings, or at least their frontages, have survived into the 21st century. On Wednesday 12 June 1937, the Coronation Day of King George VI and Queen Elizabeth, AOG 641 is standing in a near deserted New Street outside Boots between Temple Street and Bennett's Hill beneath the banners and flags; many people will be using the day off work to listen to the event on the radio, although for those living in the London area live television pictures will be broadcast from Alexandra Palace. The

bus is working on the 9 service to Quinton, but on this day appears to have very little work to do. Parked opposite the bus is a little forward-control Fordson van, while in the distance is another Corporation bus and a Midland Red single-decker. *Birmingham Central Reference Library*

651 (AOG 651)

Below One of the 20 members of the 1935 batch of BRCW-bodied COG5s not to be rebodied with a body of the same style was AOG 651; instead in February 1945 it received the earlier 1934 BRCW body from 575 (AOB 575), and

remained in service in that condition until the last day of 1947. In August of that year it is obviously not intended to work much longer with its worn-out body, and is creaking its way up Broad Street towards Five Ways on the 6 route to Sandon Road at the Bearwood boundary, while a brand new West Bromwich-registered Fordson E83W travels into the city centre. The bus is alongside the gentleman's outfitter Austin Beeny and a rather careworn Ford 7Y 8hp car that looks as if it has had a fairly hard time during the war years. Ahead of it is an Austin van parked outside Brown & Burgess's grocery shop. *Author's collection*

655 (AOG 655)

Below The 3A terminus was in Ridgacre Road, having been extended on 13 January 1937 to the junction on the dual carriageway at World's End Lane. By March 1948, what had been open fields and farmland until just 20 or so years earlier was now a rapidly expanding suburb, leaving a few of the old farmhouses hanging on to ever-decreasing parcels of land. The Victorian building on the corner of World's End Lane was at this time being used as a religious meeting centre. Bus 655 (AOG 655) is waiting at the Bundy Clock with its wooden bench, on which waiting passengers could sit in either the biting cold winter winds or the rain, sleet or snow, cursing the lack of shelter and the exposed site. Such weather was very common in Quinton, which, although just above the tiny tributary valley of Bourn Brook, was around 620 feet above sea level. *Author's collection*

668 (AOG 668)

Bottom The art of stopping a bus in the middle of the road was frequently a well learned one, especially if the bus driver had been recently transferred from a tram. Bus 668 (AOG 668), with its second BRCW body acquired as early as April 1942 from bus 670, loads up in Victoria Square in early 1946 when working on the 12 service to Bartley Green by way of Harborne. As Harborne was never served by trams, the bus reigned supreme from September 1904 when the Birmingham Motor Express Company (later BMMO) began competing with CBT's horse buses. With the expansion beyond War Lane in Harborne towards California and Bartley Green, the initial 12 bus service began on 29 January 1923 with single-deckers from opposite the Duke of York public house, and was so successful that it was extended into the city from 14 April 1926. Parked in front of the portico of the Council House is a December 1938-registered Austin Twelve, and pulling out to overtake it is 579 (AOG 579), a 1934-registered Daimler COG5 that will follow 668 as far as Five Ways before travelling along Hagley Road to Portland Road. Bus 579's original 'waistrail-less' MCCW body had been replaced by the later version from bus 598 in 1945. On the right is Christ Church Buildings, which accommodated in its Winchester House section the booking and shipping departments for the Blue Star Line, Canadian Pacific and Royal Mail Line. In later years there was always a large, beautifully made model of its latest ship in Canadian Pacific's window. *Author's collection*

674-688 (AOG 674-688)
Daimler COG5; Gardner 5LW 7.0-litre engine; NCME H26/22R body; es 3.1935-5.1935; all converted to H30/24R 1935; w 10.1945-11.1948

The body contracts for the last 20 Daimler COG5 buses ordered for delivery in the spring of 1935 were awarded to manufacturers outside the West Midlands, and this first batch of 15 were the only Northern Counties bodies built for BCT. Although they conformed to the style of the previous MCCW and BRCW bodies, they could be easily identified by having particularly thick

upper saloon corner pillars. This was not so noticeable from the front, but the front side window was extremely short. The cowl under the windscreen was a neatly rounded pressing rather than the more usual sharper-edged ledge.

682 (AOG 682)

Above right The metal-framed NCME body was a good attempt at the standard pre-war Birmingham outline, but by 1948, after 13 years of service, the lower saloon waistrail has developed a distinct old-age sag. The Corporation appears to be determined to get the most out of No 682 (AOG 682) as it is working on the anti-clockwise outer ring of the Outer Circle 11 route, unloading opposite the King's Head in Lordswood Road. In the corner of the pub's car park is a Ford 7W Ten Tudor saloon; this has

nothing to do with Henry VIII, but is a corruption of the words 'Two Door'. *E. Chitham*

683 (AOG 683)

Below The black-painted radiator of 683 is a reminder of the recently finished hostilities. The bus is unloading its passengers at the terminus of the 10 route in Quinton Road West in 1948. Note the upstairs thick corner pillar of the NCME body; that company's forthcoming standard design had a very rounded front dome that resembled the rear dome and crucially had thick corner pillars, and one wonders if it was a throw-back to the influence of the BCT specification. Behind AOG 683 is the Monarch public house, while behind the elaborate lamp standard on the rather narrow dual carriageway is the row of shops including Mason's butchers shop. *E. Chitham*

689-693 (AOG 689-693)
Daimler COG5; Gardner 5LW 7.0-litre engine; Short H26/22R body; es 2.1935; all converted to H30/24R 1935; w 10.1945-11.1948

The last five of the 100 bodies ordered in 1934 were built by Short Brothers, which until 1932 had been one of the principal suppliers of bus bodies to Birmingham. Shorts had been building bus and coach bodies since just after the end of the First World War. Throughout this period the company retained its interest in the aircraft industry, and in 1935, despite a full order book and excellent reputation, it decided to go back to full-time aircraft production, concentrating on large flying boats – like the famous S25 Sunderland, which first flew on 16 October 1937 – and four-engined bombers such as the S29 Stirling. Consequently these five Daimler COG5s were some of the last Short Brothers bodies to be built.

690 (AOG 690)
Below These buses were housed at Harborne Garage, so were employed on the Hagley Road and Quinton services as well as turns on the 11 Outer Circle service. In 1940 AOG 690, fitted with a full set of headlight masks, stands at the bus stop outside Greys department store in Bull Street when working on what was by now the 3 service shortworking to Queens Park only. Short Brothers' decision to return exclusively to aircraft manufacture was a loss to many operators: the metal-framed body was well proportioned, and these five buses could easily be distinguished by the upper saloon guttering at the front and sides. This gave the front a less 'heavy' look, coupled with the well-rounded corner pillars and long front dome side windows. Edward Grey's store was opened in 1926 when this upper section of Bull Street was widened to 80 feet, and it had a 'solid' feel somehow lacking in the more grandiose Portland-stone-faced Lewis's store built directly opposite in 1929. Greys had a comparatively lucky escape in late October 1940 when a bomb exploded in front of the shop, killing several people and leaving a large crater just in front of where 690 is standing. In 1973 Greys sold out to Debenhams, and by the end of the 1980s the building had been demolished. Behind 690 is bus 1114 (CVP 214), a 1937-registered Daimler COG5 working on the 33 route to Kingstanding. *Birmingham Central Reference Library*

691 (AOG 691)
Bottom Bus 691 was the first in the fleet to have a complete repaint after the end of the Second World War, and these five Short-bodied buses were the last to be fitted with an Autovac above the bonnet on the bulkhead. No 691 is standing at the 11 route bus stop outside Cotteridge tram depot in Pershore Road on 14 July 1945, opposite George Mason's grocery shop occupying the prestigious corner site in Watford Road. The garage also marked the terminus of the 36 tram route, where crews could be changed if required. Just visible behind the bus is 1928 Short-bodied bogie tram 818, about to work back along Pershore Road to Navigation Street. Once loaded up, AOG 691 will pull across Pershore Road, turn into Watford Road and proceed towards Bournville and Selly Oak. *J. E. Cull*

42-61 (AOP 42-61)
Daimler COG5; Gardner 5LW 7.0-litre engine; MCCW B34F body (Contract 91); es 5.1935-6.1935; all converted to ambulances 8.1939 and located at Tennant Street Garage; returned to service 12.1944-8.1946; w 5.1950-9.1950

In purchasing these 20 single-deckers, the Corporation was able to begin disposal of the Guy 'Conquest' C's; although their conversion to forward control was fairly successful, their Guy petrol engines were exceedingly thirsty. On the General Manager's advice, the chassis were standardised on the Daimler COG5 single-deck version, with a wheelbase of 17ft 6in for its 27ft 6in body length, as opposed to the 16ft 3¼in of the corresponding 26-foot-long double-decker. The bodywork was a modernised version of the metal-framed Metro-Cammell product on the Morris-Commercial 'Dictators', with the addition of the by now beaded waistrail. One bus was fitted with the optional five-speed gearbox for airport transfer work

46 (AOP 46)
Top right The arrival of all 35 single-deckers by the beginning of October 1935 enabled two new single-deck bus services, 26 and 27, to start on the second day of that month. On Monday 9 May 1938 AOP 46 waits in Vicarage Road just beyond the junction with the distant shopping centre in High Street, Kings Heath. It is about to leave on the 26 service between Kings Heath and Bristol Road, Bournbrook, by way of Dog Pool Lane, Stirchley. Residents of Dads Lane municipal housing estate now had their own bus service, albeit ten years after its completion. The large house on the right is typical of those built to the west of All Saint's Road and Vicarage Road during the last 15 years of Queen Victoria's reign. A mixture of superior villas, detached and semi-detached houses and even terraces spread away from the main Alcester Road into the countryside, which survived the onslaught of local authority-inspired suburbia until well into the 1920s. *Author's collection*

51 (AOP 51)
Above right The bare, leafless boughs of the trees in Hamstead Road and Handsworth's Parish Church of St Mary dwarf the solitary bus and the lady pedestrian. Protected by its stout brick wall, the church is in the 19th-century Decorated Gothic style, but contains remnants of most of the previous 11 ecclesiastical buildings what have stood here since 1200. Its other claim to fame is that it is the final resting place of three of Birmingham's 18th-century industrial giants – Matthew Boulton, William Murdock and James Watt – giving it the epithet 'the Westminster Abbey of the Industrial Revolution'. Travelling towards Handsworth Wood on Thursday 4 February 1937, 20-month-old Daimler AOP 51 is about to cross the Belisha crossing just north of Church Hill Road, off to the left. Still fitted with sidelights on either side of the destination box in the front dome, it is working in the 2 service, an extension of the original 10 route, which operated between the Ivy Bush and the Friary Road junction with Handsworth Wood Road, Browne's Green, near the top of Hamstead Hill. The 2 route was inherited from BMMO on 4 October 1914, and between 1923 and 1926 was extended into the City Centre. By the time the COG5s were delivered in June 1935, it had been operating to Hamstead as the 2A for more than three years, but was discontinued on 25 September 1939, and never re-instated. *Birmingham Central Reference Library*

54 (AOP 54)

Speeding along Chester Road on 15 September 1937 is COG5 54 (AOP 54) working on the 28 route, whose complicated history included running over part of the defunct Bolton Road 22 tram service and absorbing part of the inter-suburban 21 route. The new service began on 2 October 1935 between Station Street and Kingstanding, by way of Small Heath, Bordesley Green, Washwood Heath and practically everywhere else,

encapsulating in a parabolic arc all points of the compass except west! No 54 has just crossed the railway bridge at Castle Bromwich station, opened by the Midland Railway on 10 February 1842 (the elaborate multi-coloured brick building seen here was first used in 1901) and closed in 1965 with the withdrawal of passenger services to Walsall. To the right of the bus and behind the station is the site of the British Industries Fair, a sort of 1930s National Exhibition Centre, which during that decade rivalled some

of the giant European trade extravaganzas. Beyond was Castle Bromwich airfield, opened before the Great War and closed in 1958; here the Supermarine Spitfires and Lancaster bombers, manufactured on the Kingsbury Road 'Nuffield' shadow factory site to the left of the railway line, were tested and flown out to their intended RAF squadrons. The BIF buildings succumbed during the Second World War not to bombing but to the reduced needs of aircraft production and testing, being finally demolished in the 1970s as the Castle Vale housing estate was being completed. *Birmingham Central Reference Library*

62-76 (AOP 62-76)
Daimler COG5; Gardner 5LW 7.0-litre engine; Strachan B34F body; es 8.1935-10.1935; all converted to B30 perimeter + 20F 1943-45/6; w 7.1946-9.1950

For the remaining 15 single-decker bodies, Birmingham surprisingly went to Acton-based coachbuilder Strachan, which produced a body very similar to that provided by MCCW, though there were minor differences around the cab. Nos 65/67/72/75 were commandeered by the War Department

for Army service between 5 June and 1 November 1940, and 63/69/72/75/76 were painted grey during the war.

62 (AOP 62)

The 23 single-decker service was introduced in basically its final form on 21 February 1934 and served West Heath, Kings Norton, Cotteridge and Borrowdale Road, Northfield, until the closure of the Pershore Road and Bristol Road tram routes on 5 July 1952. In about 1949 bus 62 (AOP 62) travels towards Kings Norton village from Cotteridge along the tree-lined dual carriageway of Pershore

Road South. Its roof is still painted grey, done as an air-raid precaution in the first days of the Second World War, and has just crossed the River Rea, which is hidden by the trees on the central reservation. Also hidden is the medieval manorial Hurst Mill, which, although much rebuilt, ground corn as a commercial enterprise until the early years of the war. On the right, the Ford Anglia EO4A is coming out of Melchett Road, the main service road into the Kings Norton Industrial Estate, which was beginning to be developed about this time. *Birmingham Central Reference Library*

73 (AOP 73)

Above This offside rear view shows the neat design that included a full destination box and the central emergency door; perhaps the only antiquated feature was the 'D'-shaped rear windows, first seen on the Guy 'Conquest' Cs. Daimler AOP 73 is working on the 26 service from Kings Heath to Bournbrook via Dads Lane on 16 November 1948, and is outside George Mason's grocery and provision store in Bristol Road. Next door is James Broome's greengrocery shop, while behind the pollarded tree is Arthur Green's hardware shop. This part of Selly Oak between Elliott Road and Oak Tree Lane was developed at the end of the 19th century as terraced housing, but most were converted to shops before the First World War, turning Selly Oak into an important suburban shopping centre. These Strachan-bodied buses were really thrashed during the war, as all were converted to perimeter seating for 30 plus 20 standing passengers. Together with the newer BOL-registered buses, they bore the brunt of all-day single-deck bus operation in the city throughout the war. *J. E. Cull*

76 (AOP 76)

Above right Bus 76 (AOP 76) stands outside Strachan's Acton factory just prior to delivery at the end of September 1935. This Daimler COG5 was the last of the batch and is included to show the pristine condition in which all buses

were delivered to the Corporation. All the 1935 double- and single-deck buses were delivered with the sidelights mounted in the front dome alongside the destination box, but all were converted to the standard layout within two years. These buses were among the last to be delivered with the BCT patented horizontal windscreen wiper system developed by T. Rowland, the Chief Engineer, and H. Parker, his deputy, better known for their 'RP' brake adjusters; the system had two chain-driven blades held in place by the large metal frame over the windscreen. It worked very well, having been standard issue since the 1929 'Regents', but was superseded by the later simpler method of one blade sweeping an arc from a centrally mounted spindle. *Author's collection*

32-41 (BOL 32-41)
Daimler COG5; Gardner 5LW 7.0-litre engine; MCCW B34F body (Contract 113); es 2.1936-3.1936; all converted to ambulances 8.1938-2-3.1940; all impressed by Army 6.1940-11.1940; returned to BCT and converted to B30 perimeter + 20F 1942-45/6; w 4.1950-9.1950

These ten buses were to the same specification as the previous 42-61 class of 1935, but were the first in the fleet to have flexible engine mountings, which virtually stopped any engine vibration.

34 (BOL 34)

Top This is what George Cadbury must have had in mind when he began to follow the ideas of Ebenezer Howard and his 'garden city' movement: tree-lined roads, houses with gardens, individually styled semi-detached or blocks of four houses designed by a splendid architect called Harvey, and roads named after trees, were all to be found in Bournville. On its way to West Heath in 1946, bus 34 (BOL 34), still retaining its wartime grey roof, has just left Bournville Village Green in Linden Road and is travelling down Woodbrooke Road on the 27 route. *Author's collection*

36 (BOL 36)

Middle BOL 36, of February 1936, turns out of Cartland Road into Pershore Road, Ten Acres, on its way to Hay Green when working on the 27 route. Just beyond the trees on the left is the gaunt, white-pillared front of the 1931 Pavilion Cinema, while in the foreground are the tram tracks for the 36 route to Cotteridge. It is 16 July 1950, only a fortnight before 36's withdrawal from service, which coincided with the entry into service of the 30 new Leyland 'Tiger' PS2/1s, which would wipe out all the pre-war single-deckers. The bus has just negotiated an original Belisha crossing; the 'zebra' stripes would not appear until 1951. *G. F. Douglas, courtesy of A. D. Packer*

38 (BOL 38)

Bottom On 2 May 1949 the Corporation introduced a new bus service linking the airport at Elmdon with the city centre at Queen's Drive, which ran through New Street Station. Elmdon, now known as Birmingham International, was opened on 8 July 1939 by HRH Marina, Duchess of Kent, on a day that was so foul that the aircraft for the flying display never even took off. It cost £360,000, but Birmingham initially received little value from it as civilian flying ceased on 16 September 1939 and did not resume until 8 July 1946, exactly seven years to the day after its official opening. Loading up in a service road in the middle of a railway station was not ideal, so a new purpose-built air terminal was opened in Easy Row in October 1951. When the airport bus route was first introduced, two pre-war Metro-Cammell-bodied Daimler COG5s were used, as the new post-war buses were another year away; Nos 53 of 1935 and 38 of 1936 were specially overhauled and fitted with roof-mounted route-boards for the service. In 1949 BOL 38 stands just beyond the canopy over the lowest section of Queen's Drive with a new Jowett Javelin four-door saloon parked behind it. *S. N. J. White*

**694-743 (AOP 694-743)
Daimler COG5; Gardner
5LW 7.0-litre engine;
MCCW H26/22R body
(Contract 90); es 5.1935-
7.1935; converted to
H30/24R 1935; 716
rebodied BRCW H30/24R
1942; 727 rebodied EEC
H28/24R 3.1943; 23 of class
swapped bodies 1942-49;
w 3.1947-6.1950**

This was the last year of double-decker body orders with a lower seating capacity of only 48, and some buses were experimentally fitted with trafficators. The 1935 deliveries of both double- and single-deckers had their sidelights mounted on the front middle blue band and on the rear offside next to the destination box. Nos 720/21/27/30 were painted grey during the war.

710 (AOP 710)

Top right The opening up of the land beyond Alcester Lanes End in the 1920s and the reluctance of the Corporation to extend the tram route from 'The Knob' to the city boundary at the Maypole meant that the semi-express 17 route across the city to Erdington was introduced on 19 March 1928, which in turn became the 35 route southbound and the 17 northbound on 17 August 1936. The large Maypole public house was opened exactly a month before this route renumbering, and both of the parked buses are virtually new, having entered service on 1 June 1935. The

nearest, with its destination blind changed for the return journey to Erdington is 710 (AOP 710), while the other, 708 (AOP 708), still displays the 35 southbound route blind. Although the Maypole is a listed building, it was closed in 2002 and purchased by Sainsbury's, which was building a giant supermarket on the opposite side of Maypole Lane. The latest proposal at the time of writing is that the building becomes a garage! *Commercial postcard courtesy of A. Maxam*

716 (AOP 716)

Above right Profits from the Municipal Gas Department enabled the Council to build the Museum & Art Gallery, designed by H. R. Yeoville Thomason who was also responsible for the adjacent Council House. It opened in 1889 and, rather summing up Victorian civic philosophy, contains a stone inscribed 'By the gains of Industry we support Art'. Birmingham is known for its a splendid collection of pre-Raphaelite paintings by such notable artists as Ford Madox Brown, John Millais, Holman Hunt, Edward Burne Jones and Dante Gabriel Rossetti, but by 8 May 1944, when this photograph was taken, they had long since disappeared into safe storage. An empty AOP 716 runs into the city in Congreve Street prior to taking up its duties on the 32 route, while on the right is 679 (AOG 679), one of the previous year's NCME-bodied Daimlers, unloading its passengers on the 3A service from Quinton. Between the two, the design of the cab apron, below the windscreen, has changed from the well-rounded shape on 679 to the squarer one on 716, although even this was complicated as 716 had been rebodied in April 1942 with a 1936 BRCW body from 842. *Birmingham City Transport/Kithead Trust*

744-793 (AOP 744-793)
Daimler COG5; Gardner 5LW 7.0-litre engine; BRCW H26/22R body (744-785), H30/24R body (786-793); es 5.1935-8.1935; 744-785 converted to H30/24R 1935; 765 rebodied EEC H28/24R 1943; 27 of class swapped bodies 1942-49; w 2.1947-2.1950

These 1935 BRCW bodies had their sidelights mounted on the front middle blue band and on the rear offside next to the destination box; the driver's door and cab window were shorter, and the front bulkhead in the lower saloon was thicker, as were the upper saloon front corner pillars, compared to the Metro-Cammell order of 1935. Nos 752/65 were painted grey during the war.

763 (AOP 763)

Above Hagley Road West, from around Gateley Road to the Hollybush public house, became a dual carriageway in the 1930s when the new semi-detached houses were being sold for about £425. The row of Victorian houses on the left were part of a much large cluster around the junction with Quinton Lane, which also included the Red Lion public house on the hill towards Quinton village. On the extreme right is the almost new Hollybush pub of 1937, replacing a smaller building on Hollybush Hill. On 26 September 1938 AOP 763, working on the long-established 9 route, travels past the first of the newly built Hollybush shops as it prepares to climb Hollybush Hill towards Wolverhampton Road and the Warley Odeon. *Birmingham Central Reference Library*

765 (AOP 765)

Below left Daimler COG5 AOP 765 received one of the English Electric bodies intended for Manchester Corporation, and re-entered service on 19 May 1943, painted grey, remaining in that condition until the end of June 1949 when it swapped bodies with 1269; thus 765, numerically the earliest of the COG5s to receive a Manchester-style body, went to the scrapyard with a nine-year-old BRCW body. In about 1948 765 is standing at the Hawthorns terminus of the 72 route on the Handsworth and West Bromwich border. These stylish bodies were intended for a batch of COG5 chassis that were destroyed when Daimler's Radford Works was destroyed in an air-raid. The English Electric bodies were designed with Manchester's streamlined livery in mind, but they also had a neat cab apron, which was an integral part of the body, whereas on Birmingham's standard COG5 body it was part of the chassis and 'floated' separately from the body. By the time the bodies were mounted on Birmingham chassis, that neat apron had gone, replaced by the Birmingham type of apron front and rubber sealing strip. Thus the buses had swept-down windows that were attractively followed by the upper deck bands of Birmingham's livery. *R. A. Mills*

789 (AOP 789)

When the 44 tram route was abandoned on 5 January 1937, the replacement bus service was extended from the 'village' along Warwick Road to the junction with Olton Boulevard East, which had been the terminus of the former 30 Olton route until replaced when the 31 service was introduced on 24 September 1930. Passing Holy Souls Roman Catholic School and the Convent of Our Lady of Compassion is AOP 789, from Acocks Green Garage, one of the first eight COG5s to have the larger H30/24R seating layout from new, rather than the generously spaced 48 seats of earlier buses. In about 1938 it is travelling along what was then the only section of dual carriageway in Warwick Road; although only about a quarter of a mile long, it had been opened in three stages, starting near the Dolphin public house in 1932 and completed here in 1938. The bus is working on the 44 route towards the city centre and is also carrying a radiator slip-board emphasising that it will be travelling along 'WARWICK ROAD'. At the end of the dual carriageway was the large and attractive Red Lion public house, which had two large front rooms behind two generous lead-lighted window bays on either side of a classically styled entrance portico. Demolished in 1982, it was replaced by a new pub in the rear gardens of the older building. *Author's collection*

94 (BOP 94)
Daimler COG5; Gardner 5LW 7.0-litre engine; MCCW H28/24F body (Contract 105); b 11.1935, w 31.10.1950

This was the Daimler exhibit at the 1935 CMS, and was demonstrated to Birmingham from 27 August 1936 until purchased on 30 November 1936. Its MCCW body had a forward entrance with a sliding door, and a streamlined curving rear profile. It was contemporary with the metal-framed bodies (Contract 106) built for Midland Red's 150 SOS FEDDs of 1935. No 94 was purchased to gain experience with

the forward-entrance operation that Midland Red was finding so successful across its huge empire. It spent its entire life working from Acocks Green Garage on the 1 and 1A routes, where it amassed almost 270,000 miles. For four years it was used on these two routes with AEC 'Q' No 93 (AHX 63), which had a different front entrance position.

94 (BOP 94)

Just about to pull away from the wartime bus stop and shelter in St Mary's Row, Moseley, on Friday 5 May 1948, the day when news broke that General Jan Smuts had resigned as Prime Minister of South Africa, is BCT's only forward-entrance pre-war double-decker, 94 (BOP 94).

The driver, having already pre-selected first gear, waits to get the two bells from the conductor before climbing away from the Moseley Road junction towards the Tudor St Mary's Church, Moseley's parish church from 1853. Behind the bus, on the far side of Moseley Road, is the steeply gabled parade of shops built in around 1907 on land belonging to Moseley Hall. Opposite St Mary's Row and running down a steep hill towards Edgbaston is Salisbury Road (named after Queen Victoria's last Prime Minister), which is still lined with a goodly selection of 'Arts & Crafts' housing dating from just after the road was cut in 1899. May 1948 was a low mileage month for 94, as it only ran 1,152 miles. *T. J. Edgington*

94 (BOP 94)

This unique bus is about to turn into College Road from Stratford Road, Springfield, on 27 July 1950, on a shortworking to the College Arms at the bottom of nearby Shaftesmoor Road, prior to turning back and heading for Acocks Green. It has just crossed the River Cole bridge, opened on 15 May 1899, and is standing almost exactly where the terminus of the Stratford Road steam trams had been located; CBT's College Road depot was where the photographer is standing. Behind the bus, next to the old fire alarm box, is the start of a row of terraced tunnel-back housing in Knowle Road dating from about 1905. No 94 was demonstrated to Birmingham after being idle for over eight months, which was surprising as it had been especially built for Birmingham, with as many of the undertaking's standard fixtures and fittings as possible. It had three lower saloon rear windows, the middle one being part of the central emergency exit, while mounted above these windows was an impossibly high rear destination box. The conductor stands in the forward entrance wearing his leather satchel and Bell Punch ticket machine. The sliding door was never used and was held in the open position from its very early months in service – can you imagine a BCT conductor, whose job description had caused the Corporation to adopt a destination display that would not need to be changed at an inner terminus, taking on an extra duty by shouting 'Moind the doer'? *L. W. Perkins*

794-843 (BOP 794-843)

Daimler COG5; Gardner 5LW 7.0-litre engine; BRCW H30/24R body; es 7.1936-11.1936; 814/20/42 rebodied EEC H28/24R 1942; 34 of class swapped bodies 1944-49; 794/801/06/16/32/38 rebodied MCCW H30/24R 1947-48; w 5.1948-12.1960

These first 50 buses of the 1936 contract were built by BRCW of Smethwick, with bodies that had several features that distinguished them from the Metro-Cammell version, but generally they were not as long-lived. Nos 815/27-30/37-42 were painted grey during the war.

805 (BOP 805)

Opposite top Having turned right from Edmund Street into Congreve Street, 805 makes a bee-line for the bus stops just out of view on the right facing Victoria Square. This area of central Birmingham was the heart of the city's administration; Yeoville Thomason's Renaissance-styled Council House on the right was completed in 1879 and adjoins the portico entrance of his Museum & Art Gallery; at its Edmund Street corner, where the soldier is standing behind the bus, is the tall clock tower known locally as 'Big Brum'. On the other side of the distant Edmund Street is the Council House Extension, opened in 1912 but not completed until 1919. In 1951 BOP 805 is working on the 9 service from Quinton by way of Hagley Road and Broad Street, carrying a body acquired from 812. Despite its apparent good condition, these BRCW bodies were not as substantial as their Metro-Cammell cousins, being more prone to remedial bulkhead repairs; the former were easily distinguishable from the latter by having thicker upper saloon corner pillars. No 805 would be taken out of service on New Year's Eve 1952 when its tax or CoF were due; eventually it served about a year as a snowplough. *S. E. Letts*

814 (BOP 814)

Opposite middle Rosebery Street was the Corporation's second purpose-built tram depot, opening on 14 April 1916 with a maximum capacity of 85 tramcars. Despite losing the Dudley Road trams on 30 September 1939, it was not allocated any buses until May 1947, just a month after the closure of the 32 Lodge Road tram service, though the Ladywood 33 service soldiered on from the depot until 30 August 1947. BOP 814 was the bus blown over by a bomb blast in Queen Street alongside Highgate Road Garage on 19 November 1940. As its nearside lower saloon was very badly damaged and repairs would be lengthy, it was selected as the first bus to be fitted by Metro-Cammell with one of the recently purchased English Electric bodies intended for

Manchester Corporation; it returned to service on 1 January 1942. Having just left the garage in about 1959, it pulls up the rise in College Street towards Spring Hill to start its latest duty. The wall on the left belongs to part of the Victorian housing in the Spring Hill-Icknield Street area, which included some of the city's grimmest back-to-back courtyards. *B. W. Ware*

836 (BOP 836)

Bottom The 55A bus service was the direct successor to the former 8 tram route, though it had been reduced to a shortworking of the 55 bus route to Shard End. It turned around at the island at the Pelham Arms, a 1920s mock-Jacobean council estate public house that stood at the junction of Alum Rock Road and Pelham Road; an early post-war Standard 14hp car is parked outside. The tarred-over tram tracks were those of the terminal stub of the Alum Rock tram route, abandoned on 30 September 1950. In 1951 BOP 836, by now carrying the body from 841, which it acquired in October 1948, stands with its crew at the Bundy Clock prior to returning to the city. Next to it is the single-storey Co-Operative grocery store, with pyramids of cans neatly stacked in the windows, while almost hidden by the bus is the Co-op butchery department. *E. Chitham*

844-893 (BOP 844-893)
Daimler COG5; Gardner 5LW 7.0-litre engine; MCCW H30/24R body (Contract 122); b 7.1936-9.1936; 27 of class swapped bodies 1944-49; w 7.1948-8.1954

These was the second half of the 50 buses delivered in the autumn of 1936. The earlier vehicles had been delivered new as part of the initial allocation to Liverpool Street Garage, opened on 16 September 1936, while the later ones were allocated to work on the Inner Circle from Barford Street. They were different from earlier COG5 double-deckers by having flexible engine mountings, which gave a much smoother ride. Nos 888-893 were painted grey during the war.

844 (BOP 844)

Above On Thursday 20 June 1946, with post-war austerity rapidly taking over from the euphoria of victory, the parked cars in Colmore Row would be a delight to any modern-day car enthusiast! On the right is one of the first two-tone six-cylinder Austin 14/6s of late 1937, while behind that it is a Hillman Minx Phase 1 and a 1939 Birmingham-registered

Wolseley Ten, which, with its 1140cc ohv engine, cost £215. Parked outside the Bradford Permanent Building Society offices on the left, being passed by bus 844 (BOP 844) on the 7 route, are a 1946 Austin 8hp saloon and a pre-war Morris Eight Series II. This part of Colmore Row has always been the financial heart of Birmingham, though it was a 'no man's land' as far as bus stops were concerned,

with services speeding between the distant St Phillip's Cathedral and the adjoining quiet haven of the Church Yard and the phalanx of bus stops in Victoria Square. The bus still has a grey and khaki roof, but by now is carrying the body from 874, which it obtained in October 1944. The cross-city 7 route to Portland Road was introduced on 26 September 1927; in the background, working another cross-city service, the 15A to Barrows Lane, Yardley, is Leyland 'Titan' TD6c 246 (EOG 246), whose 1939 Metro-Cammell body was built without a front rain shield as well as having slightly taller upper saloon front windows. *Birmingham Central Reference Library*

883 (BOP 883)

Opposite bottom   Turning out of Gerrard Street into Nursery Road is 883 (BOP 883), which entered service on 1 September 1936. It is about to pull up at the first bus stop in Nursery Road, on the corner of Berners Street, working on the Inner Circle 8 route on its way to Hockley. The intending passengers are pupils and their domestic science teacher from nearby Lozells School, who are going on a picnic in a park, although the nearest one on this route was about 3 miles away at Chamberlain Gardens, Edgbaston. They are doing a course in 'Home Organisation' and the school owned one of the adjoining houses so that the girls could be taught how to make beds, wash clothes, sweep floors and cook meals. *Birmingham Central Reference Library*

894-963 (COH 893-963)
Daimler COG5; Gardner 5LW 7.0-litre engine; MCCW H30/24R body (Contract 139); b 11.1936-1.1937; 901 rebodied BRCW H30/24R 1941; 918 rebodied EEC H28/24R 1942; 912/27 fitted with MCCW top decks from Morris 532/20 in 1941 and 1940 respectively; 46 of class swapped bodies 1941-49; w 10.1948-12.1960

This was the largest order yet placed for a single batch of buses, and the 70 were delivered in time for the first day of bus operation after the conversion of the Stratford Road, Warwick Road and Stoney Lane tram routes on 5 January 1937. Seven bus routes had 'over-run' the 'main-line' tram routes, but with expensive track renewals becoming due, the decision was made on 7 July 1936 to replaced the trams, and the new buses were operated from Acocks Green and Liverpool Street garages until that at Highgate Road was re-opened in June 1937 after its conversion from trams at a cost of £6,500. Nos 918/20-25/34 were painted grey during the war.

898 (COH 898)

In June 1947 the Inner Circle bus route was diverted away from Highgate Road because of road works and ran along Woodfield Road, Ombersley Road and into Ladypool Road. Rather battered-looking COH 898, with its BRCW bodywork in dire need of a repaint, turns into Ombersley Road with its equally run-down late-Victorian tunnel-backed terraced housing. The elderly couple on the left are passing the Methodist Chapel and behind them is the three-storey 'Mozart Works', the home of the Sames Piano Company until a succession of fires caused by sparks from passing steam locomotives on the old Midland Railway bridge put an end to it. On the right of the bridge are the signals at the end of the long-deserted Camp Hill & Balsall Heath station, closed on 27 January 1941; although the line is still in use, the station buildings have long since disappeared. *A. N. H. Glover*

914 (COH 914)

Above The 14 route was first operated from the Alum Rock tram terminus at the Pelham public house on 13 December 1933 as far as Flaxley Road, but was extended to the city on 13 October 1937 and further into the suburbs of Kitts Green and Lea Village on 21 September 1938. The distant mock-Jacobean Glebe public house, dating from the mid-1930s, stood at the junction of Glebe Farm Road and Kitts Green Road and seemed to dominate all the roads leading to

it like a medieval church, being built on the highest spot for miles and taller than the surrounding council houses. COH 914 is working into the city on the 14E route in Audley Road; the roads in the Kitts Green municipal estate were made of concrete, but the dark patch of asphalt marks damage caused by a bomb. *Commercial postcard*

918 (COH 918)

Middle Standing at the Hawthorns terminus in Holyhead Road at Camp Lane in 1947, almost opposite the old South Staffordshire Tramways Hawthorns depot, is bus 918 (COH 918). Damaged in 1940, it was fitted with this H28/26R body in May 1942 until it passed to 1228 (FOF 228); the remains of the body were still recognisable in Kallis Lefkaritis's yard in Larnaca, Cyprus, in 1986. No 918 is working on the 72 route, introduced on 2 April 1939 when the West Bromwich tram services were replaced by Birmingham and West Bromwich Corporation buses. Originally all-over grey, by 1947 only the roof and the rear dome are still so painted. *R. A. Mills*

926 (COH 926)

Bottom What at first sight seems to be an ordinary Metro-Cammell-bodied Daimler COG5 is far from that! The top deck is from Metro-Cammell-bodied Morris-Commercial 'Imperial' 520, and this combination was fitted to 927 in December 1940 and transferred to 926 in February 1946. It is working on the 9 route in Hagley Road, Bearwood, and has just crossed Bearwood Road, having left the bus stop alongside Lightswood Park. It is passing the row of late-Victorian shops that by 1948 included Bobette's hairdressing salon owned by Miss Betty Partridge, while behind the bus, with its canvas sunblinds pulled down, is James Weston's tobacconist shop. Except for the body framing in the upper and lower saloons not matching, this body combination is quite attractive, with the upper saloon front corner pillars being much narrower than on post-1933 Metro-Cammell deliveries. Perhaps only the lack of upper saloon mouldings beneath the painted blue bands between the decks looks a little odd. In this guise COH 926 lasted until November 1949 before being taken out of service. *S. E. Letts*

961 (COH 961)

Camp Hill was a major staging post on the many bus routes that used Stratford Road. In February 1944 bus 961 (COH 961), which entered service on 1 January 1937, swings around the traffic island in front of the Ship Hotel when working on the 44 route to Acocks Green. In the distance, travelling through Camp Hill, is 904 (COH 904), one of Highgate Road's Daimler COG5s. The Victorian public house on the corner of Camp Hill and Sandy Lane had the strange sub-title 'Prince Rupert's Headquarters – 1643', a reference to a minor skirmish between Royalist Rupert and Parliamentarians nearby at Easter, April 1643. Confusingly, the area's name has nothing to do with Prince Rupert's 'camp', but is a

corruption of Kempe Hill, named after the local 15th-century landowners. Following the bus is a Dorset registered Leyland lorry, and partially hidden by the traction pole with the 'Please Cross Here' sign is Birmingham Corporation Service Vehicle 59 (EOJ 459), a Morris-Commercial T3 van. The photograph was taken from the wooden-braced brick parapet in Stratford Road next to Camp Hill Goods Station. *Birmingham Central Reference Library*

**964-968 (COX 964-968)
Leyland 'Titan' TD4c;
Leyland 8.6-litre engine
with torque converter
gearbox; Leyland H28/26R
body; es 5.1937, w 9.1948-
12.1948**

This batch of five buses was bought in order to find an alternative to the Daimler COG5 for the 1939 tramway abandonments on the Handsworth-West Bromwich-Dudley and Dudley Road-Smethwick-Oldbury-Dudley routes. They were fitted with the Lysholm-Smith torque converter, trialled by Birmingham on the TD2c demonstrator 94 (TF 7310), as well as on some converted AEC 'Regents'. The buses were simplicity itself to drive, being well suited to tram motormen converting to buses, with a two-position floor-mounted lever in place of a gear lever: forward for the variable torque converter, and back for the direct gear that was available at about 20mph, the equivalent of fourth or top. The bodywork was of the latest style, designed by Colin Bailey who had left Metro-Cammell with the brief to sort out the mess at Leyland's body plant concerning its 1933 'Vee-front' six-bay metal-framed body. The result was this sleek five-bay design, which, with modifications, would be the basis of all future Leyland double-deck bodies until the company ceased building bus bodies in 1954.

964 (COX 964)

Although seen before, this photograph of COX 964 is one of the few taken of these five Leyland 'Titan' TD4cs in service. The first of Colin Bailey's new Leyland-bodied buses entered service in March 1936, and Birmingham's five arrived exactly 14 months later. The bus is turning out of Islington Row into Five Ways when working on the Inner Circle 8 service in May 1938, when the order was announced for 85 'Titans' for the conversion of the Hockley, West Bromwich and Dudley group of tram routes. To the left, between the bus and the National Provincial Bank, is the late-Victorian Five Ways Clock, while on the right is Lloyds Bank on the corner of Calthorpe Road, built in 1909 to the designs of P. B. Chatwin and attractively faced in white Portland stone. *Author's collection*

965 (COX 965)

Photographs of these buses with Birmingham Corporation are very rare, so although very 'bussy' and blurred this one does show enough of 965 (COX 965) to be included. It is in Bradford Street, passing the tile-and-terracotta-fronted Anchor public house of 1902 before turning left into Rea Street, working on the 15 service to Church Road, Yardley, when these new buses were first allocated to Liverpool Street in 1937. The rear dome was rather square, which would give way to a more rounded style in late 1937, and although not perpetuated with the remaining pre-war bus orders, the single emergency rear window would become the post-war standard for BCT. *J. E. Cull*

968 (COX 968)

These five Leyland TD4c chassis were sufficiently modified so as to be virtually to the TD5 specification. The body, although little modified from the standard Leyland outline, incorporated many of the normal BCT design features, including liberal amounts of chrome. The buses incorporated a standard Birmingham straight staircase, and even the standard swivel windows of the driver's cab. They were in competition with five AEC 'Regent' 0661s, and with Birmingham's need to 'dual source' its future bus fleet orders, the Leylands were cosseted for the duration of the comparative trial period during the second half of 1937; as a result, perhaps against expectations and logic, they won! They had quite short lives with Birmingham, living out an 11-year service life before being perhaps prematurely withdrawn in 1948 and sold off quickly for further use. *Leyland Motors*

483 (DOB 483)
AEC 'Regent' 0661; AEC A168 four-cylinder engine; Short H27/21R body (1.1931) ex-AEC 'Regent' 483

This was an AEC demonstrator from March 1937 to April 1938, fitted with a four-cylinder oil engine that effectively created a 'Regent' 4 chassis for trial with BCT. It had the 1931 Short 'piano-front' body from 483 (OV 4483), so it looked virtually the same as these earlier buses, although it had the shaped front wings covering the chassis dumb-irons that were AEC standard equipment about this time. It was later rebuilt and sold with a new Park Royal body as DAA 848. There is no known photograph.

969-1033 (COX 969-999/CVP 100-133) Daimler COG5; Gardner 5LW 7.0-litre engine; MCCW H30/24R body (Contract 144); es 5.1937-8.1937; 976 rebodied BRCW H30/24R 1949; 978 rebodied EEC H28/24R 1949; 1018 rebodied EEC H28/24R 1941; 42 of class swapped bodies 1941-52; w 10.1949-12.1960

This was another order for 65 of the by now standard Daimler COG5s with MCCW bodies. They were ordered to augment the existing bus fleet, for although there were no new routes opened at this time, there were a large number of route extensions into suburbs such as Weoley Castle, Lea Hall and Kingstanding. No 987 was painted grey during the war. No 1018 was used as the 1937 Illuminated Coronation bus, and 1022 as the Festival of Britain float, 1951.

971 (COX 971)

Above Standing in Albert Street on 12 May 1950 is a 1949 Ford Prefect 10hp E493A four-door saloon, and beyond it is 971, one of ten COG5s that entered service on 1 May 1937. It is waiting to pick up passengers outside the Beehive independent department store, which sold everything from electrical goods to ladies' frocks. It closed on 29 February 1972 and with it went its wonderful brass canisters and cables used to send money, receipts and bills to and from the sales floor. It is a little over seven months since the Moseley Road tram abandonment and, instead of one of the brand new Daimler CVD6s, COX 971 is working on the 50B route to Alcester Lanes End. In the distance is 1235 (FOF 235) with the prototype post-war body constructed by Brush in 1946 and mounted on a Daimler COG5. It is on a shortworking back to Liverpool Street Garage and stands on the tram tracks that by this time were only being used for journeys to or from Kyotts Lake Road Works in Sparkbrook. *R. T. Wilson*

973 (COX 973)

Above right 'Save today – to save tomorrow' was one of the wartime propaganda slogans carried on the buses, and in about 1941 COX 973 waits opposite the Hawthorns. On the right is a metal advertisement for E. Rudd, a nameplate

manufacturer based at 19, Soho Hill, just up the hill from Hockley bus garage. The bus is fitted with wartime headlight masks and appears to have had the white edging paint recently applied. It shows the infamous 'SERVICE EXTRA' destination blind, though the Metro-Cammell-bodied Leyland 'Titan' TD6c parked in the distance has the more helpful 'HAWTHORNS 72'. *R. T. Wilson*

1008 (CVP 108)

Below After any tram route abandonment, most of the recoverable infrastructure was removed fairly quickly, but where anything could be re-used it was saved and renovated. In Hockley Brook, near Hockley tram depot and the point where the former CBT cable trams changed cables, the tram shelters for outbound Corporation trams were re-sited in the throat of Claremont Road at an angle to Soho Hill. Painted green and generally refurbished, the sturdy shelters, built as recently as 1935, served the out-of-town bus services in Hockley until the building of Hockley Flyover began in late 1965, when the whole community and shopping centre were swept away. All the shops on the left, including Orchard's shoe shop, beneath whose awning the lady is purposefully striding, and Hawkins's gentlemen's outfitter shop, were demolished. In the background are the earlier mid-19th-century buildings around Hunter's Road and Hockley Hill. In 1958 Hockley Garage had nine of the overhauled 41 Daimler COG5s that were brought back into service to cover a shortfall in peak-hour bus availability. The driver of 1008 (CVP 108), which was used as a snowplough between November 1954 and April 1958, waits for the brand new Ford Popular 100E car to pass in late 1960, before travelling to the Oxhill Road terminus. The 70 route was opened on 2 April 1939 to replace the 26 tram service, though it was extended from the tram terminus at Rookery Road to the Uplands Hotel, a distance of about 600 yards. *Author's collection*

1021 (CVP 121)

Below left It might seem surprising to the present-day generation that during the Second World War life went on as normal, but here is evidence! Pedestrians, shoppers, children and military personnel walk along the bomb-damaged High Street in 1944, which had lived an uneventful life until the night of 9 April 1941 when all the buildings from the extreme left around the corner into New Street were destroyed. In future years this huge area of derelict land became known as the 'Big Top' site, after a series of large marquees were erected there. Behind the bus are the remnants of High Street's eastern-side shops, which had survived the bombing. The gap behind the bus is where Marks & Spencer's bazaar was located, while the modern square block on the corner of Carrs Lane is the late-1930s premises of Jay's furniture store. The driver of 1021 walks in front of his bus before getting into his cab and driving off to Yardley Wood railway station in Highfield Road on the 29 service. Approaching High Street from Dale End is what appears to be a Hillman 14 of 1938 vintage. Parked outside Slater's & Bodega's wine merchant is bus 1021 (CVP 121), a Daimler COG5 that unusually managed to operate a full 14-year life without undergoing a body swap. *Birmingham Central Reference Library*

1023 (CVP 123)

Above In August 1937 immaculate one-month-old bus 1023 (CVP 123) crosses the Navigation Street junction when travelling into the city along Hill Street on the 15A service from Barrows Lane, Yardley. As a Midland Red SOS QL turns into Hill Street, the Corporation bus, with its bonnet lined out in gold paint and its sparkling chrome radiator, is also carrying a radiator slip-board, which could be altered to give extra information to intending passengers. It was a different age for travellers in those days, when every bus was immaculately clean and running on time, electric tram wires spanned the streets, and it cost 12 shillings by train to London, with the added bonus of not only being pulled by a steam locomotive, but also arriving on time! *G. H. F. Atkins*

1024 (CVP 124)

Above right One of the strange things about the five-cylinder Gardner-powered Daimler COG5s was that, once under way, with a power-to-weight ratio almost exactly the same as the post-war Daimler CVG6, they performed and sounded virtually the same. Pulling away from the traffic lights in Warwick Road at the Baker Street/Golden Hillock Road junction is 1024, one of the few pre-war buses to remain in continuous service. It has just passed what was always known as 'the Bomb Building Site' on the right between Baker Street and St John's Road, Greet. Despite its age, 1024 (CVP 124) is working on the 44A route during 1959 and is loaded to the gunwales. Perhaps its driver's desire to pick up as many passengers as possible has caused the following Guy 'Arab' IV, 2576 (JOJ 576), also working on the 44A route, to catch up – or, in driver's parlance, 'Let the b— in front do all the work!' *R. F. Mack*

1034-1038 (CVP 134-138)
AEC 'Regent' 0661; AEC A173D
7.585-litre engine with AEC pre-selector
gearbox; MCCW H30/24R body
(Contract 145); es 7.1937-8.1937,
w 3.1949-1.1951

This batch of five buses was bought in order to find an alternative to the Daimler COG5 for the 1939 tramway

abandonments on the Handsworth-West Bromwich-Dudley and the Dudley Road-Smethwick-Oldbury-Dudley routes. They had AEC pre-selector gearboxes with a Daimler-type quadrant mounted on the steering column. All were rebuilt during the early months of the war with flexible engine mountings.

1035 (CVP 135)

Top In 1937, new bus 1035 (CVP 135) speeds away from Five Ways in Islington Row having just passed the entrance to Bath Row. This was the second of the five delivered in July 1937, allowing the Corporation to undertake comparison trials with the five Leyland 'Titan' TD4cs delivered two months earlier. All five were allocated to Liverpool Street Garage, from where they operated until withdrawal. It is passing the Be Be See Hotel having just overtaken a parked Morris Eight van, as it runs down the hill towards Bristol Street, working on the Inner Circle route. *J. E. Cull*

1036 (CVP 136)

Middle In Lee Bank Road, having climbed the hill from Sun Street West, virtually new CVP 136 has just passed a parked early 1930 Morris-Commercial 1-ton pick-up van and the distant three-storey terraces that formed the street frontages of a myriad of courtyards and back-to-back properties. These terrible houses were swept away in the early 1960s when Lee Bank became one of Birmingham's five comprehensive development areas, to be replaced by even more socially divisive multi-storey blocks of flats – but that is nearly 30 years and a World War away! On this sunny summer day in 1937, the bus passes Wheeleys Road as it approaches Five Ways, working on the Inner Circle route. *J. E. Cull*

1038 (CVP 138)

Bottom The last of the five 'Regent' 0661s, 1038 (CVP 138), lasted nearly two years longer than the earlier four, not being sold until January 1951. Looking in fine fettle, it stands opposite the Fox & Goose public house in Washwood Heath Road on a special duty, perhaps a school playing-field contract. It is the summer of 1950 and a 762 class bogie tramcar stands in the central loading island prior to returning on the 10 route to Martineau Street in the city centre. These MCCW bodies were virtually the same as those on the contemporary Daimler COG5s, but the curved bottom to the windscreen softened the 'heavy' look of the front dome in the upper saloon; the large expanse of cream down to the front numberplate, coupled with the chromed radiator, also helped. *T. J. Edgington*

1039-1138 (CVP 139-238)
Daimler COG5; Gardner 5LW 7.0-litre engine; MCCW H30/24R body (Contract 144); es 8.1937-11.1937; 1133 rebodied EEC H28/24R 1941; 1097/1120 rebodied EEC H28/24R 1949; 63 of class swapped bodies 1941-50; w 3.1949-12.1960

This was a continuation of the previous Metro-Cammell contract for standard BCT bodies mounted on Daimler COG5 chassis, and many of this batch were the chosen for refurbishment during their 'Indian Summer', which in some cases lasted until the final day of 1960. No 1113 was painted grey during the war, and 1116 was used as a VE Day float in 1945.

1054 (CVP 154)
Above Although it is a sunny 23 August 1939, it would not be too much of a cliché to state that the war clouds are gathering as two-year-old 1054 (CVP 154) leaves the 44 terminus and heads towards Acocks Green village. This section of Warwick Road had only been widened in August 1938, and the block of shops, including Halford's cycle shop, just visible through the trees on the central reservation, had replaced a large Victorian 'pile' called Eastbourne House in about 1936. *Author's collection*

1060 (CVP 160)
Above right Looking very smart, CVP 160 pulls away from the bus stop in Thomas Street at the bottom of Leopold Street in about 1959, working on the 49 route into 'town' – no one ever referred to it as 'the city' any more than anyone other than professional 'Brummies' ever called themselves a 'Brummie'! In the distance is the 1 in 13 climb up to Moseley Road, which was considered sufficiently steep that, in 1913, the 401 class four-wheeled trams were equipped with the Spencer & Dawson air and oil brake, only used elsewhere in the hilly city of Bradford, where Messrs Spencer and Dawson held the positions of General Manager and Chief Engineer. Overtaking the bus is a Vauxhall Velox EIP saloon of June 1956. Off to the right were the St Martin's flats, centred on Emily Street; this Eastern European-inspired development was completed in 1939 after three years' construction and consisted of 267 balconied three- and four-bedroom blocks. They were a warning to future urban redevelopers that in the late 1950s was not heeded, and by the early 1960s they were being termed 'a rundown warren of problem flats'. They were demolished in 1981 and many of the 1960s Highgate Comprehensive Development Area properties, such as those being built on the left, have also met the same fate. *R. F. Mack*

1070 (CVP 170)

Above Harborne High Street was saved from the clutches of the tramcar by the Gough-Calthorpe family's refusal to allow them to work through those parts of Edgbaston that they owned. As a result CBT horse bus operation ruled these two suburbs until a new company, called Birmingham Motor Express, began motorbus operation on 12 April 1904 between New Street and the Bear Hotel at Bearwood. As explained in the introduction, the early buses suffered from the poor road surfaces and unreliability problems, and in 1907 the motorbus service ceased operation. It was not until May 1912 that BMMO re-introduced motorbuses, and again the Hagley Road and Harborne routes were targeted,

this time successfully. Buses severely damaged the financial viability of the Harborne Railway, originally an LNWR. branch line, and it closed for passengers on 26 November 1934. Working along High Street, Harborne, in 1952 on the 3A route, the direct descendant of the original BMMO service to Harborne, which became the Corporation's 3 route to Ridgacre Road in October 1914, is bus CVP 170, which has just passed the clock tower of Harborne's first Board School, by this time the area's main junior mixed school, opened in 1881 to the designs of local architects Martin and Chamberlain. Post-war Daimler CVA6 bus 1552 (GOE 552) is about to pass the impressive building on its way into the city also on the 3A route. *E. Chitham*

1096 (CVP 196)

Left When the 10 tram route was abandoned on 1 October 1950, the replacement bus service was the 56 route, which went along Coleshill Road to the Clock Garage on the corner of Newport Road. The 56B was the direct equivalent of the tram route, as it turned back at the Fox & Goose public house. CVP 196 loads up with passengers in about 1953, working on what by now was a regular shortworking of the Newport Road service. On the right is the Beaufort Cinema, a distinctive-looking Tudor-styled picture house designed by Hurley Robinson. On opening in August 1929 it had a wonderful two-manual Compton electric organ, which later found its way into the EMI studios in St John's Wood, London. The Beaufort was demolished in 1978 and replaced by a new shopping complex. *C. Martin, courtesy of K. Lane*

1107 (CVP 207)

Above The 1937 Daimler COG5 chassis of 1107 (CVP 207) was fitted with the 1939 body from 1216 in December 1950, making it one of the very last body swaps undertaken by the Corporation at Tyburn Road Works. The 1938 and 1939 bodies were built by Metro-Cammell and could be distinguished by their deeper front upper saloon windows and the lack of guttering over them, which gave these later buses a more modern appearance. No 1107 is loading at the top of Albert Street, working on the 50 service to the Maypole via Moseley and Kings Heath. It is about 1959, during 1107's 15-month return to service together with 40 other COG5s that were either taken out of store or returned to traffic after being used as snowploughs. It was quite unusual for these elderly buses to carry advertisements at this time, but 1107 is displaying one for the long-forgotten Payne's GP tea. The bus was bought for preservation by Barry Ware in 1964 and happily is still in active order at the BaMMOT Museum at Wythall. *R. T. Wilson*

1115 (CVP 215)

Above right One of Perry Barr Garage's 1958 allocation of seven Daimler COG5s, 1115 (CVP 215) unloads its passengers outside the Hollybush public house in Hagley Road West in about 1960, working on the long cross-city 34 service from Kingstanding to Quinton. On the other side of the dual carriageway, a Standard Vanguard Phase 1 speeds passed the Hollybush shopping parade as it travels into the city centre, while a Morris J2 van is about to overtake the bus. No 1115 received the body from 1083 in 1948 when it came in for its first major post-war overhaul, and like many of the batch had been sent to Samlesbury Engineering of Samlesbury near Blackburn for renovation. Like all the COG5s that were put back into front-line service in 1958, 1115 has been given the Tyburn Road treatment, and although it only remained in service until the end of December 1959, it looks extremely smart, belying its 22 years! *A. D. Broughall*

1139 (DON 439)
Daimler COG5; Gardner 5LW 7.0-litre engine; MCCW H30/24R body (Contract 173); es 12.1937, w 4.1954

This bus was exhibited at the 1937 CMS and would have been bus 101, numerically the first bus of the 1938 contract, though

it received a body built to the earlier 1937 style. It was allocated from new to Liverpool Street Garage, where it stayed for all its BCT career.

1139 (DON 439)
The only Daimler COG5 bus to have an 'odd' registration was 1139, which it was allocated because of its unusual early history. A decision was made by Daimler that one of its Metro-Cammell-bodied Birmingham buses should be exhibited at the 1937 Commercial Motor Show at Olympia, so an extra chassis was built. As a result, the next batch of 50 chassis was reduced by one, so that 101 (EOG 101) never existed and the 1938 deliveries from Metro-Cammell were apparently one short, starting at 102. No 1139 was duly exhibited but with a body style from the 1937 batch, retaining the guttering around the front upper saloon windows that was omitted for the first time from the EOG-registered buses. DON 439 consequently looked like one of the CVP batch, except for the external guttering being left out just below the middle blue livery band. It was rebodied with the standard Metro-Cammell body from 1128 in November 1948, and in about 1950 it is standing in Hob Moor Road near the Green Lane junction in Little Bromwich, quite close to the City Sanatorium Hospital, working on the 16A cross-city service to Handsworth Wood. *D. Barlow*

102-150 (EOG 102-150)
Daimler COG5; Gardner 5LW 7.0-litre engine; MCCW H30/24R body (Contract 195); es 9.1938-11.1938; 12 of class swapped bodies 1946-50; w 2.1949-6.1954

This was the class of 50 Metro-Cammell-bodied COG5s that was missing its first member –see 1139 above. These bodies incorporated some subtle differences from the 1936-37 vehicles, which considerably modernised their appearance. When new they were allocated to Liverpool Street Garage,

although in later years many of the survivors were running out their time from the 'home of the geriatric Birmingham bus', Birchfield Road Garage. They were supposedly numbered in this series for accountancy reasons, presumably being bought out of capital rather than the revenue account. Nos 102/04-07/09/11 were painted grey during the war.

107 (EOG 107)
The imposing red brick and an even darker red terracotta General Hospital was built to the design of W. Henman between 1894 and 1897, with rows of round-topped

elliptical windows, polygonal towers and steeply pitched roofs like a strangely shaped church nave. Much of the tiling was made by Doulton in Rowley Regis. There always seemed to be a dark, brooding presence about the hospital, especially on gloomy days like this in the winter of 1948, as bus 107 (EOG 107) pulls away from the stop at the bottom of Steelhouse Lane. It is working on the 5A service to Perry Common, which was extended to Court Lane from Enderby Road on 24 July 1939. In 1998 the old 'General' was re-opened as the Princess Diana, Princess of Wales, Children's Hospital. *G. F. Douglas*

111 (EOG 111)

Above The once thriving area behind New Street station in the vicinity of Hurst Street, Smallbrook Street and Station Street was swept away in the late 1950s as part of the then exalted Inner Ring Road scheme. What it did was to destroy a large commercial area of the city centre and leave it to either decay in a long lingering death on the wrong side of the new elevated road, or worse still be demolished. The impressive four-storey premises of George Hull, wholesale drysalter and paint and varnish merchant, stood on the corner of Hurst Street and Smallbrook Street and was to fall victim to demolition in early 1957. Bus 111 (EOG 111) slows to a halt

behind tramcar 434, one of the 1912 batch of 50 UEC-bodied 54-seat open-balconied trams mounted on Mountain & Gibson 7ft 6in trucks. The tram is picking up passengers in Hurst Street just short of Smallbrook Street, where the Pickford's pantechnicon is speeding. It is making one of its last journeys on the 37 service to Cannon Hill Park by way of Balsall Heath, as this is Saturday 1 October 1949, when all the tram routes operated by Moseley Road depot were abandoned. One of only seven of the class painted grey during the war, 111 is working on the 15B route to Garretts Green Lane. Noticeable on these 1938 buses are the larger rear windows in both saloons. *J. S. Webb*

121 (EOG 121)

Above right The original 21 bus service was introduced on 19 November 1930 as a single-deck-operated route to the Tyburn

House public house at the junction of Tyburn Road and Kingsbury Road. After various extensions, in October 1935 it became a shortworking of the 28 route, which was extended as the 28A in May 1948 from the Kingstanding Road-Hawthorn Road junction down the very steep hill in Dyas Road, Great Barr, to a turning area at the mouth of Glenmead Road, within 100 yards of Aldridge Road. This part of Great Barr had been taken into the city in 1928, and within a decade the former farmland had been built over with a mixture of private and council housing. In May 1948, bus 121 (EOG 121), which entered service in September 1938, stands at the Dyas Road terminus. Behind it are 1131 (CVP 231) and 1065 (CVP 165), similar vehicles but dating from 1937, which is evident from the guttering over the front upper saloon windows, a feature that was omitted on the 1938 bodies. The 21 route last operated on 13 February 1955. *R. Knibbs*

151-200 (EOG 151-200)
Daimler COG5; Gardner 5LW 7.0-litre engine; BRCW H30/24R body; b 10.1938-1.1939; Nos 151/52/55/61/66/77/79/86/88-90/200 rebodied MCW H30/24R 1949; 15 of class swapped bodies 1948-49; w 4.1949-8.1954

These represented the usual BRCW share of the year's orders and again were both subtly different from previous ones as per the improved specification and BRCW's interpretation of those alterations. When new, all 50 were allocated to Yardley Wood Garage. Nos 151-161 were painted grey during the war.

1162 (FOF 162)
Below In 1952 and 1953 Birmingham City Police became increasingly worried about congestion in Digbeth at both the Moat Row and Rea Street junctions, and made photographic surveys at both points to help with the traffic arrangements that were to come into place when the road-widening scheme, delayed by the war, was completed in 1955. Although a police photograph, this might have been a publicity shot for Fordson, with an E83 10 cwt van sandwiched between a 1949 Thames 3-ton tipper and, going out of the city, another Thames Luton van about to cross the redundant tram lines at the Rea Street junction. Following the tipper is bus 1162 (FOF 162), working on

the 29A route to Baldwins Lane, Hall Green. Curiously, this route had both of its cross-city termini outside the city boundary; after unloading at the Baldwin public house, buses did a 180º turn around a traffic island, part of which was in Solihull, while at the Kingstanding end the terminus was in Collingwood Drive, about half a mile into Aldridge. Behind the bus is one of the 2626 class of Daimler CVD6s introduced in July 1951 to replace the trolleybuses along Coventry Road, although this one, which has just passed Digbeth's Civic Hall, is on the 60 route to Cranes Park Estate, previously not served by the 'silent servants'. On the left is the forecourt of Midland Red's Digbeth Garage, where BHA 334, a 1936 SOS FEDD with a Metro-Cammell body, a BMMO S8, also bodied by MCCW in 1948, and an EHA-registered FEDD, but with a Brush H30/26F body of 1938, are some of the buses parked on the cinder-covered area. Going into Birmingham is 1605 (GOE 605), a 1948 Daimler CVG6 with a Metro-Cammell H30/24R body, working on the 37 route from Hall Green. *Birmingham Central Reference Library*

177 (EOG 177)
Opposite above Travelling along Colmore Row on Thursday 20 June 1946 is EOG 177, which still has its grey and khaki camouflaged roof. The BRCW bodies could always be easily distinguished from the front by their taller front windows, thinner upper saloon corner pillars, a more pronounced squarer shoulder to the ledge below the windscreen, and an

extra lip all around the canopy, which can be seen here below the destination box and to the right of the windscreen. No 177 is working on the 24 service to Daisy Farm and Warstock, introduced on 19 November 1930 to branch from the Stratford Road tram route and gain access to the southern edge of the Yardley Wood area, where council housing development on what had been farmland until after the end of the Great War had begun in the late 1920s, with some 712 houses being built there adjacent to the Solihull boundary. The bus is passing on the right a 1937 Middlesex-registered Packard Super Eight and the previously seen two-tone six-cylinder

1937 Austin 14/6s, while parked outside Lloyds Bank's Colonial and Foreign Department is a 1939 Standard Flying Twelve saloon. *Birmingham Central Reference Library*

188 (EOG 188)

Below The summer of 1939 was a very pleasant one as far as the weather was concerned, though storm clouds to the south were gathering at an alarming rate. The trees in full leaf make for a tranquil, almost melancholic scene, in view of what was to come! By this time Wake Green Road, crossing from left to right, and the distant Yardley Wood Road were surrounded by lavish 1890s upper-middle-class detached and semi-detached villas in the Wake Green area at the eastern end of Moseley, built on the Grevis family

acres when their land was part of the Worcestershire parish of Yardley. (Wake Green is derived from an Anglo-Saxon word 'waca', a village green where an annual festival was held.) Occupying one of these large houses, visible through the trees on the right, was Moseley College, an educational establishment for young ladies run by the Misses Amy Pole and Maud Tonkyn. EOG 188 is travelling along Yardley Wood Road towards Warstock on the 24 service, while heading into town are a Morris Eight 5 cwt van, a rather smart-looking Wolseley Series II 25hp saloon, first registered in August 1937, and a Morris-Commercial C-type lorry. On the left, having almost jumped the traffic lights, an elderly Austin Sixteen totters around the corner into Wake Green Road. *Birmingham Central Reference Library*

188 (EOG 188)

Below The western side of Carrs Lane above the Corner public house was destroyed in the April 1941 air-raids on the city centre; the pub, with its mock wooden frontage, stands beyond the far bus shelter and above the mid-1930s Rover 14 saloon. For many years the gaping holes left by the bombing were fenced off with advertising hoardings, such as the two in front of the bus for Domestos bleach and Walls's sausages, products that are still brand leaders today. At the Theatre Royal in New Street, Charles Boyer, Charles Laughton, Cedric Hardwicke and Agnes Moorhead are appearing in G. B. Shaw's philosophical charade *Don Juan in Hell*, which Laughton was directing – what a cast! The play opened on 25 June 1951, with a box costing 100 shillings (£5) and a seat in the balcony just 5 shillings. The trolleybus wires of the inbound loop on Carrs Lane's gradient for the Coventry Road service have only this week left in use as the trolleybuses are to be withdrawn on the last day of June. EOG 188 is one of Acocks Green Garage's Daimler COG5s that had originally been fitted with BRCW bodies, but 118 now carries the 1939 Metro-Cammell body taken from 1153 in November 1948, which it will keep until withdrawal in May 1954. It is working on the 44A route. *E. Chitham*

189 (EOG 189)

Bottom On 17 September 1949 EOG 189 is working the semi-express, limited stop 35 route to the Maypole. This gave people who lived beyond the Alcester Lanes End tram terminus, where tramcar 423 is standing on the 42 route to Albert Street, an quick but expensive journey home. The bus is about to pull away from the stop opposite 'The Knob', correctly the King's Arms, rebuilt in this mock-Tudor style in 1911. It had originally been a Holders pub, whose brewery was based in Nova Scotia Street, near Coleshill Street, and an early acquisition by Birmingham brewer Mitchells & Butlers, in 1919. Parked on the left is a 1949 Austin A40 Devon four-door saloon, the first new post-war model to come out of Longbridge. No 189 has the 1937 MCCW body from COH 917, identifiable as an earlier body by the rain strip around the front upper saloon windows. Cut down to a single-decker, 189 later saw service with Lefkaritis in Cyprus. *A. N. H. Glover*

5.
1939–1942
WARTIME DEVELOPMENTS

This was a time of huge bus fleet expansion, despite the ominous developments in Europe, with 265 new buses being delivered by March 1940, but with the closure of the two tram routes that went outside the city boundary and into the Black Country. The lease period on the tram tracks to West Bromwich, Wednesbury and Dudley via Soho Road and the services to Bearwood, Soho, Smethwick, Oldbury and Dudley were due to expire on 1 April and 30 September 1939 respectively. In the case of the former, agreement was made with the neighbouring authority in 1924 that Birmingham would take over the operation of the tram services from the South Staffordshire Tramways (Lessee) Company on a 'manage and control' basis on behalf of West Bromwich Corporation. The termination of the agreement was brought forward to 31 December 1938, but decisions were made too late, deliveries were slightly delayed and initially BCT had to dissuade the West Bromwich management from purchasing trolleybuses, even though it had raised the height of the garage at Oak Lane to accommodate the proposed overhead. Consideration was also given to retaining all the tramlines within the Birmingham boundary as the trackwork was still in good condition, but it was finally decided to have a jointly worked bus service. Based on the results of the 1937 trials for dual-sourcing bus chassis, Birmingham ordered 85 Leyland 'Titan' TD6c chassis with Metro-Cammell bodies at a total cost of just over £2,000 per bus, and all of them were available for service from the newly converted Hockley Garage on the first day of bus operation. West Bromwich Corporation supplied 31 Metro-Cammell-bodied Daimler COG6s as its share of the service. The strange anomaly was that until 27 August 1967, passengers crossing the boundary at the Hawthorns had to pay separate fares on each side.

During 1939 another 97 Metro-Cammell-bodied Daimler COG5s with Metro-Cammell bodies were purchased, as well as the last pre-war Daimler COG5s carrying some of the last BRCW bodies to be manufactured. Again BCT was beginning to explore the purchasing of bus bodies from a third source, and bought one-off prototypes from English Electric, Park Royal and Brush. Further attempts to purchase chassis from another source were curtailed by wartime restrictions, although 15 AEC 'Regent' 0661s were provisionally ordered, but of course never materialised.

The second tramway closure was that of the Dudley Road group of routes, which occurred on 30 September 1939, after many hastily arranged discussions regarding the advisability of the closure in view of the declaration of war on 3 September 1939. The state of the track, particularly around Brades Village, Oldbury, was awful, and the local authorities would not countenance the retention of the tramcars any longer. Despite these closures, all the 59 four-wheel trams that had been used on the route were stored where they stood in Rosebery Street and West Smethwick depots in case the tram service might have to be re-instated, although there was to be no reprieve and they were all broken up by the spring of 1940. At the last minute, the Lodge Road (32) and Ladywood (33) tram services were given a stay of execution in order to conserve fuel, as at least here the trackwork was in reasonable condition. The trams to Bearwood (29), Soho (31), and Oldbury and Dudley (87), as well as all the shortworkings, were withdrawn and replaced by a group of bus services jointly worked with BMMO (Midland Red), all the services being prefixed with the letter 'B'. The year 1939 also saw the final withdrawal of the 71 class cars and the last of the former CBT trams. Birmingham purchased another 50 Leyland 'Titan' TD6cs with Leyland bodies, numbered 1270-1319, specifically for the replacement Dudley Road bus services, making them the last delivery of pre-war buses.

The Nechells trolleybus 7 route was 'temporarily' closed on 30 September 1940 and replaced by buses because of blackout problems from the use of a skate on the track to return the current in order to get the trolleybuses from Washwood Heath depot to the nearest point on the route at Bloomsbury Street; it was never re-instated. In the next seven months, bombs caused damage to trams, trolleybuses and buses; most of the buses in Highgate Road Garage were extensively damaged on 19 November 1940, and even more disastrously at Hockley Garage, where 19 buses were burned out, another four only slightly less damaged, and a staggering 88 damaged. Yet only six were written off!

211-295 (EOG 211-295)
Leyland 'Titan' TD6c; Leyland E39/4 8.6-litre engine with torque converter gearbox; MCCW H28/24R body (Contract 196); es 12.1938-4.1939; 211/51/79/87/89 destroyed by enemy action 11.1940; 214/15/17/25/31/35/37/41/49/59/73/93 rebodied EEC H28/24R 1942 and all painted grey during war; six buses swapped bodies 1948-49; normal withdrawals 1.1949-2.1954

The entry into service of 1236 in January 1940 marked the arrival of the last of the Daimler COG5s with Metro-Cammell bodies. The English-Electric-bodied COG5 1237, and 1238 with a Park Royal body, both entered service on 1 March 1940, being the only vehicles to enter service during that year; no new buses were delivered for the next 22 months. This was despite the withdrawal of two AEC 'Regents' and seven Morris-Commercial 'Imperials' in 1939 and 1940. The final deliveries consisted of four 8-foot-wide Daimler COG6s intended for Johannesburg, which could not be delivered because of German U-boat activity, and six 'unfrozen' Leyland-bodied Leyland 'Titan' TD7s and two further TD7s, one with a Park Royal body and one with an NCB body, both to MoS 'Utility' design. All of these buses were delivered between December 1941 and July 1942, and marked the end of buses designed before the Second World War.

The 'Titan' TD6c was developed to meet BCT specifications and introduced BCT's policy of 'dual sourcing' its chassis. These 85 buses were purchased expressly for the conversion of the Handsworth, West Bromwich, Wednesbury and Dudley group of tram services. The TD6cs were effectively the new TD7 model with the Lysholm-Smith torque converter gearbox. They were fitted with flexible-engine mountings and worm-and-nut steering, and had large-diameter flywheels that virtually eliminated any vibration, even at tick-over. The seating capacity of the Metro-Cammell bodies was reduced by two in the upper deck because of the added weight of the torque converter gearbox.

231 (EOG 231)
Left The original Wheeler Street tram service had opened as far as Villa Cross on 20 November 1912, while the loop around Hamstead Road to Hockley was completed on 8 January 1913. This formed a circular service, the 24 going clockwise and the 25 in the opposite direction. The latter was abandoned on 7 August 1933, while the 69 bus route replaced the 24 tram service on 2 April 1939, but unlike the tram service, which could stop in the middle of the road, in this case Lozells Road at the Villa Cross public house, and turn back by the driver simply changing ends, the replacement buses

had be found a turning place. This was done by using Mayfield Road, between Lozells Road and Heathfield Road, as the new terminus. In about 1951, and looking in remarkably fine fettle, one of the Manchester-style English Electric-rebodied 'Titans', EOG 231, stands in Mayfield Road, which was lined with large, late-Victorian tunnel-back housing. The MCTD-styled body was well suited to the more dignified Birmingham livery, though the swoop line beneath the 'D'-shaped lower saloon windows meant that the livery slightly failed to match the body contours. The only part of the Manchester streamlined design that was not in harmony with the rest was the two asymmetrical square-cornered rear platform windows, which looked as though the draughtsman had drawn them just before going home on a Friday afternoon. It is a great pity that one of these buses did not survive long enough to be preserved, though 237 was owned by Stevenson of Spath until January 1964 and a half-hearted attempt was made to purchase it. In the meantime, 231 was still extant in August 1987 as a chassis and a lower saloon frame in a scrapyard outside Larnaca in Cyprus. *E. Chitham*

237/262 (EOG 237/262)

Top right Having entered service on 1 February and 1 March 1939 respectively, the two buses stand on Hockley Garage's cobbled forecourt early in April 1939 immediately after the conversion of the tram service to

bus operation on the second of that month; these buses were run in at both Acocks Green and Liverpool Street before the Hockley conversions. The orthochromatic film used was not very sensitive to yellows, and makes the primrose part of the Birmingham livery look extremely dark. This extremely rare photograph shows 237, one of the 12 war-damaged buses rebodied with English Electric H28/26R bodies intended for Manchester Corporation, with its original Metro-Cammell body. It also shows both buses with nearside wing marker poles, which looked like a child's lollipop; they were broken or removed very soon after the vehicles entered service. *C. F. Klapper*

264 (EOG 264)

Above right EOG 264 is working into the city along Soho Road on the 75 route from Wednesbury in April 1939, and has just passed the Grove Lane junction, with Dudley's home furnishing shop on the far side, while immediately

behind it and the recently redundant traction pole is the imposing Soho Road branch of Birmingham's Municipal Bank. The 70 bus route to The Uplands public house in Oxhill Road made a right turn into Grove Lane before passing Handsworth Grammar School for Boys, whose towered and multi-gabled building opened in August 1862. Further down the hill in Grove Lane was the huge Handsworth Park and the Edwardian Grove Lane Baths, dating from 1907. No 264, with a 'helpful' radiator slip-board displaying 'BIRMINGHAM', stands bedecked with timetabling window posters informing the public of travel arrangements for the forthcoming Easter Holiday. The driver waits to pull away from the stop outside Charlton's gas showroom, which in later years would be occupied by the West Midlands Gas Board. In the days of locally produced coal gas, the heat from the demonstration fires in these showrooms was quite overwhelming, while the smell of gas was nauseating. *Author's collection*

273 (EOG 273)

Below On the night of 22-23 November 1940, 17 TD6cs were badly damaged when Hockley Garage was bombed, five being written off. The remaining 12 were rebodied with English Electric bodies built at the firm's Phoenix Works in Bradford that had been intended to be Manchester's 1287-1361, but 25 of them had been destroyed in an air raid on Daimler's Radford works in November 1940. All the completed bodies were delivered to Manchester's Car Works where they were stored on trestles until Birmingham purchased one in August 1941 as a trial, then an initial batch of 15, which was followed up with an order for another five in November 1941. Eight of these new bodies were fitted to Daimler COG5s, the chassis for which they had been intended, but the other 12 were rebuilt at Metro-Cammell to suit the different wheelbase of the Leyland 'Titan' TD6c. The bodies were also fitted to the Leyland chassis by Metro-Cammell at Saltley. No 273 (EOG 273) re-entered service with its EEC body on 18 September 1942 in the grey livery that was applied to all the rebodied Leylands, and during 1943 stands outside Snow Hill station in Colmore Row wearing its full wartime garb. It is working on the 72 route to the West Bromwich boundary at the Hawthorns, the Holyhead Road home of West Bromwich Albion FC, whose main claim to fame is that, at about 547 feet above sea level, it is the highest football league ground in either England or Scotland. *C. F. Klapper*

276 (EOG 276)

Bottom On 19 July 1951 bus 276 (EOG 276) has just unloaded its three passengers at the Oxhill Road terminus of the 70 route. By this date the lower saloon offside destination box has been blanked over in an economy drive to save linen; it also saved the conductor having to change four destination blinds – but remember that Birmingham's destination displays were intended not to be changed at all during a day's work. Behind the bus are some of the privately owned semi-detached houses at the bottom of Sandwell Road where it joined Oxhill Road, with its rows of late-Victorian terraced housing. The bus will do a U-turn across the end of Sandwell Road's dual carriageway and load up alongside the Uplands public house, an extremely large suburban pub opened on 16 September 1932 to the designs of architects Harrison & Cox, who had also designed the York in Hall Green, the College Arms in Springfield and the Court Oak on the Harborne/Quinton boundary. Despite its good condition, 276 was withdrawn the following April and finished its career at the fledgling Stansted Airport working for the airline Skyways. *G. F. Douglas, courtesy of A. D. Packer*

1140-1236 (FOF 140-236) Daimler COG5; Gardner 5LW 7.0-litre engine; MCCW H30/24R body (Contract 220); es 7.1939-11.1939; 40 buses swapped bodies 1944-49; 1235 rebodied Brush H30/24R 1.5.1946 (prototype post-war body); 1213 rebodied BRCW H30/24R 1947; 1150/68/85/94/1209 rebodied BRCW H30/24R 1949; 1161/1228 rebodied EEC H28/24R 1949; w 10.1949-1.1955

These were the last batch of Daimler COG5s to be delivered with Metro-Cammell bodies, which were of the improved type introduced on the EOG-registered buses of 1938, although the two glazed windows in the rear emergency exit were even larger than before. They were initially allocated to Acocks Green Garage, replacing Morris-Commercial 'Imperials'.

1143 (FOF 143)
Top right Looking towards Cotteridge on 16 April 1950, 1143 (FOF 143) is working on the 18A bus route; it has just crossed the railway bridge at Kings Norton station and is descending the steep hill in Pershore Road South, Cotteridge, where the central reservation began with its mature trees and flower beds across the deep River Rea valley. To the right is the edge of the fledgling Kings Norton Industrial Estate, opened in the late 1930s. The 18A route went between Fitzroy Road

in Allen's Cross Estate, Northfield, via Cotteridge, Kings Norton, Monyhull Hall Road and the Valley at the junction of Haunch Lane and Yardley Wood Road. It was introduced in this form on 19 November 1930 and today is still one of the few inter-suburban bus services wholly operating within the city. *Birmingham Central Reference Library*

1161 (FOF 161)
Above right The EEC H28/26R body on 1161 (FOF 161) was originally fitted to 1018 (CVP 118), but was transferred when the 1937-built bus was withdrawn in February 1949. No 1161 returned to service on 1 May 1949 with the Manchester 'streamlined' body and remained in service in this condition until withdrawn in

March 1954. Saturday 1 October 1949 was the last day of the semi-express 35 bus service to the Maypole; on the following day the 35 service would be replaced by the 50 route, which would also be part of the replacement bus services for all the Moseley Road tram routes. The bus is standing in Station Street, created in 1883 when a large area of 18th-century slum property was taken over by the Midland Railway to build its section of New Street station south of Queen's Drive. Behind 1161 is Leyland TB7 trolleybus 81 (FOK 81), going to Yardley on the 93 route; it was one of the last 12 trolleybuses purchased by Birmingham, entering service on 15 February 1940. Both vehicles will pull away and immediately turn right at the Market Hotel into Dudley Street. *S. N. J. White*

1162 (FOF 162)

Below People are milling about between Hedges chemist shop and the Belisha beacon on the corner of Witton Road as the clock on the Midland Bank on the corner of Lozells Road shows 12.32pm. Parked outside the bank is an early post-war Austin 10hp car, while bus 1162 (FOF 162), working on the 33 route, is showing the unusual destination display consisting of only the word 'KINGSTANDING'. It is overtaking Brush-bodied maximum-traction-bogie tramcar 632, which is travelling into the Six Ways area on the 6 route from Perry Barr. The bus driver has placed his charge in this position so that he can take the right fork in front of the Royal Exchange public house to travel into Alma Street. Six Ways, Aston, was one of the most complicated sections of tram trackwork in the city, with five

of the six roads carrying tramlines; Alma Street was the odd one out. In the distance, in Birchfield Road, is petrol-engined AEC 'Regent' 661, rebodied by Brush with an MoS body in April 1944. *G. F. Douglas, courtesy of A. D. Packer*

1171 (FOF 171)

Bottom The tram tracks through the centre of the important Camp Hill island, at the junction of Stratford Road, Sandy Lane and Stratford Place, were those of the former Stratford Road group of tram services, abandoned at the end of services on 5 January 1937; after that date they were only used by trams going to the nearby Kyotts Lake Road Works. Apparently 'beached' across the tram tracks, to the total disinterest of the two policemen standing close by, is green-painted Birmingham Salvage Department

motor lorry dustcart No 39, which appears to be a 1939 Morris-Commercial CV with a six-door refuse body and a very flamboyant curved-roof cab. In 1944 FOF 171, disguised to some extent by being in full wartime garb, is turning round the island in front of the Victorian Ship Inn while coming out of the city on the 13A route to Priory Road, Yardley Wood. This service was introduced on 5 June 1929 as a branch off Stratford Road in Sparkbrook using Stoney Lane to reach the new 1920s housing estates beyond Billesley. The bus is being followed by a Standard Flying Eight, a model introduced in late 1938 and continuing in production until 1940, then again between 1946 and the summer of 1948. On the extreme right, in the shadow of the derelict buildings in Sandy Lane, coming up from the 13ft 9in bridge, is a Ford AA lorry registered with an AOL mark first issued in December 1934. *Birmingham Central Reference Library*

1217 (FOF 217)

Opposite top On 28 February 1951, FOF 217 waits at the impressive shelters in Colmore Row alongside the Churchyard and St Phillip's Cathedral while working on the 1 route shortworking to Moseley. These buses were very much the 'end product' of a design first introduced in 1934, although the detailed improvements made during the intervening years produced a body that could have been post-war; only the angled windscreen and awkward ledge beneath it were a throw-back to the original pattern.

The bus is being overtaken by a JVP-registered Morris-Commercial 25 cwt van. On the left, Whitehall Chambers was the first block along from the distant Snow Hill station and Livery Street, and included the Type Writer Bureau, an office equipment company, while behind the late-1940s Rover 60 P3 six-light saloon is Greatrex's ladies' hairdresser and the National Milk Bar. *G. F. Douglas, courtesy of A. D. Packer*

1233 (FOF 233)

Middle When the 5 tram route was still operating, it shared the narrow section of Villa Road's Victorian shopping centre, between Hamstead Road on the right and the distant Villa Cross public house on the corner of Heathfield Road, with the 25, 29 and 29A bus routes. Bus 1233 (FOF 233), still sporting a wartime black-painted chrome radiator, is about to turn left at Francis Hallam's chemist shop, rumbling over the cobbles and the tram tracks in about 1949; it is operating on the 29A route to Baldwins Lane on the other side of the city at the Hall Green-Solihull boundary. *F. N. Lloyd-Jones*

1235 (FOF 235)

Bottom Bus 1235 (FOF 235), a 1939 Daimler COG5 chassis, was rebodied by Brush to the new post-war Birmingham design in 1946. The body had the usual straight staircase, but the all-metal body was fitted on the chassis with a new rubber mounting system to relieve vibration and also to lower the overall height of the vehicle slightly. Certain features were not repeated on future exposed-radiator bus body orders, such as the deeply recessed windscreen, although this would eventually return on the 'new-look'-front buses that first appeared in 1950. One peculiarity not repeated was the enormous destination boxes front and rear, which were soon replaced by normal-sized ones, and although the apertures were reduced, the large front box shape was retained as a reminder of the earlier giant lettering. Standing in Victoria Square in 1946, just beyond Waterloo Street and alongside Lyons' Tea Room, where one was served afternoon tea and cakes by black-dressed and white-frilly-aproned 'nippies', 1235 is working on the 15B service to Garretts Green Lane, which was introduced on 23 November 1938 and went about halfway along that road to Horrell Road; it was not extended until 23 January 1949, to Sheldon Heath Road, where it turned at the newly opened Garretts Green Technical College. *Author's collection*

1235 (FOF 235)

Bearwood Bus Station was opened in 1952 and used by Midland Red, West Bromwich Corporation and BCT. In 1958, bus 1235 (FOF 235) is parked near the Bearwood Road and Kings Head end of the bus station, working on the B80 shortworking to Grove Lane, one of the bus services introduced on 1 October 1939 after the abandonment of the Dudley Road tram services. The Corporation's normal share of these new routes was the B80 to the city boundary, within smelling distance of Mitchell & Butler's Cape Hill Brewery, and the B81 shortworking to Windmill Lane. The other route operated by BCT was the B83 to Soho station by way of Heath Street. The remaining routes B84 to B87 were generally operated by Midland Red, although the latter as far as Oldbury was occasionally worked by the Corporation to balance out the mileage agreements between the Corporation and Midland Red. The B82 was the 'mainline' route to Bearwood, and it was normally Birmingham buses that carried this number at Bearwood. The Grove Lane service was usually worked from the Edmund Street end of the city centre, so the use of the route number from the outer terminus back to the Birmingham boundary was quite unusual. The nearside rear reveals that this prototype post-war Brush body had the traditional BCT straight staircase, although the high-mounted rear destination box was not repeated, much to the delight of conductors of shorter stature. Another pre-war remnant was the short length of curved panelling between the rear platform bulkhead and the rear of the nearside mudguard. Unlike the later production batch, all of 1235's saloon windows had un-radiused tops and, unusually, the upper saloon seats were covered in patterned moquette rather than the usual leather cloth. The successful operation of this body, designed to have a '12-15-year trouble-free' life, led to the ordering of 100 similarly Brush-bodied Leyland 'Titan' PD2/1s, 1656-1755, which had a very protracted period of delivery, entering service between March 1948 and May 1949. *A. D. Broughall*

1236 (FOF 236)

Entering service in January 1940, some two months after the other Metro-Cammell-bodied COG5s in the FOF series, 1236 was used as a 'template' for the English Electric and Brush bodies. It had a slightly modified body from the rest of the batch, with detailed interior differences. In 1950 it is parked at the top entrance to Perry Barr Garage alongside the offices and facing Wellhead Lane. Just visible in the gloom of the garage is brand new 2015 (JOJ 15), an MCCW-bodied Daimler CVD6 that entered service on New Year's Day 1950. *J. H. Taylforth collection*

1237 (FOF 237)
Daimler COG5; Gardner 5LW 7.0-litre engine; English Electric H30/24R body; es 3.1940, w 4.1954

English Electric had been a major player in tram body building in the UK, both of traditional-looking tramcars and the more advanced metal-framed streamliners of the 1930s. This was numerically the first of the 'one-off' bodies ordered in 1939.

1237 (FOF 237)
Although English Electric had supplied Birmingham with 'piano-front' bodies on AEC 'Regents' in 1930, by the end of the 1930s it was gaining only a very small number of orders for its standard body design, which was generally of uninspired appearance. However, the one resulting from EEC's successful tender to BCT was a very attractive double-decker. The front profile was a little more upright than the standard, but was rather spoiled by the blue-painted front apron to the cab. The 'floating' cab was slightly different from normal, being marked by the bottom of the cream-painted panel beneath the windscreen. On a snowy day in 1949, the well-wrapped-up driver of 1237 approaches the Bundy Clock in Lordswood Road to peg in and continue his journey when working on Birmingham's famously long Outer Circle route. Behind the bus is the Kings Head public house, the first hostelry along Hagley Road because, rather like the Cadburys at Bournville, who were teetotal Quakers, the owning Gough-Calthorpe family would allow no drinking establishments on their land. The Kings Head replaced a much earlier inn, when the Holte Brewery's architects, Owen and Ward, produced a mock-Tudor, half-timbered, brick and terracotta building in 1905. Also parked in Lordswood Road is a 1934 Austin 10/4 saloon. *S. E. Letts*

1238 (FOF 238)
Daimler COG5; Gardner 5LW 7.0-litre engine; Park Royal H30/24R body; b 3.1940, w 7.1951

Of the three prototype bodies supplied to the Corporation, this was Park Royal's interpretation, and that firm's first body for Birmingham; the body number B5640 was allocated to this one-off vehicle. It was a faithful reproduction of Birmingham's standard body, though the body pillar design produced a somewhat thin-framed look.

1238 (FOF 238)
Loading up at the utility bus shelters in Hagley Road at Five Ways opposite the old King Edward's School buildings on Christmas Eve 1949 is 1238 (FOF 238), on its way to Quinton on the cross-city 34 route from Kingstanding. This service replaced the 34 tram on 11 August 1930, making it the third Birmingham tram route to be abandoned. The tram started in Navigation Street and went by way of Holloway Head and Islington Row to Five Ways, while the replacement bus took the more direct route along Broad Street to the outer terminus at the Kings Head, Lordswood Road. No 1238's body had the thinnest front corner pillars of any pre-war body mounted on a Daimler COG5, a rather square destination aperture and a curved profile to the area above the number plate. Inside, it was the only bus in the fleet to have metal-capped window interiors, but otherwise it was perhaps the most modern-looking body on a Birmingham COG5. *J. E. Cull*

1239 (FOF 239)
Daimler COG5; Gardner 5LW 7.0-litre engine; Brush H30/24R body; es 12.1939, w 8.1950

The third prototype body was built by Brush and its appearance was the nearest to the standard Metro-Cammell body. The only difference was the introduction of radiused saloon windows, which began to look as if it might become the standard for future orders, but of course these were among the last pre-war standard BCT bodies to be built.

1239 (FOF 239)
Having turned left from Snow Hill into Steelhouse Lane, FOF 239 is working on the 'CITY' service, the rather anonymous shortworking of the cross-city 29 route, in

1949. It is passing the decoratively fronted, late-Victorian Wesleyan General building, which would survive until 1988. Always allocated to Perry Barr Garage, its windows are radiused at the bottom with squared tops, and it is carrying an upside-down radiator slip-board; on its arrival in High Street, this will be turned round to show that the bus will be travelling towards Kingstanding. The tram is 642, one of the unique batch of 25 MRCW trams delivered in 1923, the first to be totally enclosed. It is standing alongside the silver-painted steel loading barriers while working on the 2 route to Erdington. *J. Whybrow*

1240-1269 (FOF 269)
Daimler COG5; Gardner 5LW 7.0-litre engine; BRCW H30/24R body; es 9.1939-11.1939; four buses swapped bodies 1946-49; 1258 rebodied MCCW H30/24R 1946; 1247/52/62 rebodied MCCW H30/24R 1949; 1269 rebodied EEC H28/24R 1949; w 7.1949-6.1954

These were numerically the last Daimler COG5s to be delivered, although their chassis numbers were in the same series as the 1140-1236 class with Metro-Cammell bodies. They were also, together with the 90-strong class of London Transport's N1 trolleybuses numbered 1555-1644, the last bus bodies ever built by BRCW, but were generally not very durable, with exactly half of the batch being withdrawn by 1950.

1261 (FOF 261)
With the early post-war prefabs in Colegreave Avenue in the background, FOF 261 waits at the Bundy Clock in Stratford Road, Springfield, near River Cole bridge, whose parapet is just visible on the extreme left. It was the replacement of the old hump-backed bridge that allowed the Stratford Road electric tram routes to be extended to Highfield Road, Hall Green, on 31 May 1914. The old

terminus was at the former CBT College Road steam tram depot site, just in front of where the buses are parked. The slightly more upright front and the very square ledge below the windscreen are good identification points for the BRCW body. The bus, looking freshly repainted, is working on a Five Ways shortworking of the 1 route on 1 May 1950. Drawn up behind it is five-month old 2332 (JOJ 332), a Crossley DD42/6 with a Crossley H30/24R body, working on the 1A route to the City Centre. *G. F. Douglas, courtesy of A. D. Packer*

1269 (FOF 269)
Buses reached the Warstock Estate on 19 November 1930 and travelled along the crescent-shaped Langstone and Arlington Roads to the terminus in the latter just after crossing Daisy Farm Road. Standing alongside the rows of 1920s council houses in about 1951 is the very last Daimler COG5 to enter service in Birmingham, 1269 (FOF 269), which went on the road on 1 November 1939 with the other seven of the class operating from Acocks Green Garage. It ran out its last years from Yardley Wood Garage, having been fitted with the Manchester-styled EE body from AOP 765 at the end of August 1949. Behind it, 1140 (FOF 140), the first of the 1939-delivered Metro-Cammell-bodied COG5s, has just arrived at the 24 route terminus and waits to pull up to the Bundy Clock as soon as 1269 leaves for the City Centre. *G. H. Stone*

1270-1319 (FOF 270-319)
Leyland 'Titan' TD6c; Leyland E166 8.6-litre engine with torque converter gearbox; Leyland H28/24R body; es 8.1939-11.1939; 1315 destroyed by enemy action 11.1940; 1281/83 fitted with MCCW top-decks from Morris-Commercial 'Imperials' 536/53 1941; normal withdrawals 3.1949-4.1954

These 50 buses were purchased for the Dudley Road tram conversion and were allocated to Hockley Garage to join the previous batch of EOG-registered TD6cs. They had flexible engine mountings and a large flywheel, producing a very smooth, vibration-free ride. The blend of the standard Leyland body design and BCT detail design produced one of the best-looking pre-war municipal buses in the country.

1270 (FOF 270)
On its way to the city terminus in Paradise Street, 1270 (FOF 270) storms up the hill over the cobbles in Suffolk Street working on the 95 route from Ladywood. This route replaced the 33 tram route, which had survived its proposed 1939 abandonment until 31 August 1947, and was immediately operated by the majority of the 1270-1319 class, which were transferred to Rosebery Street Garage. By late 1947 the bus looks in need of a repaint, although it still has its torque converter header tank and the lower saloon front bulkhead half-painted in the original 1939 primrose livery. It has just passed the rich red brick-and-terracotta-fronted Technical School, completed in 1895 and demolished in the late 1960s as part of the Inner Ring Road scheme. The early-19th-century buildings on the left include Leslie Brock's hairdressing salon and a coffee house that was also a tobacconist, while on the right a BRCW-bodied Daimler COG5, with its radiator still painted black, comes out of Holliday Street on its way to Weoley Castle on the 20 route. *W. J. Haynes*

1277 (FOF 277)

Above Speeding past tramcars loading at their shelters in Navigation Street is bus 1277 (FOF 277), working on the 95 service to Northbrook Street. It is 1950 and the line of trams includes 544 at the head, working on the 70 route to Rednal, and 542, on the 71 route to Rubery. This terminus, among three-storey back-to-back properties, overlooked the distant Dudley Road Hospital and the nearby deep cutting formed by Thomas Telford's Birmingham Canal of 1829 and the former LNWR Stour Valley railway line, opened in 1852 to Wolverhampton and the North West. The bus has its right-hand trafficator out, indicating that it is about to turn into John Bright Street, travelling away from the Paradise Street terminus. At the far end of Navigation Street is Suffolk Street, behind the distant hoardings, is the back entrance to the former Midland Railway's Central Goods Depot. *S. Eades*

1281 (FOF 281)

Below left Two of the 50 TD6cs, 1281 and 1283, were so badly damaged when Hockley Garage was bombed on the night of 22-23 November 1940 that urgent remedial action had to be taken to get them back into service in the spring of the following year. Both were fitted with the Metro-Cammell top-decks from petrol-engined Morris-Commercial 'Imperials'; FOF 281 received that from bus 536, but unlike the two Daimler COG5s that were similarly treated, the window frames did not mate up and the front of the upper saloon was set back, leaving almost a canopy above the front of the driver's cab. No 1281's conductress, with her Bell Punch ticket machine, talks to the Inspector who is striding purposefully towards the rear platform of her bus as it stands in Margaret Street outside the Art School in 1947, working on a B82 service to Bearwood. From this angle, the MCCW top-deck looks decidedly uncomfortably perched on the Leyland lower saloon. *R. A. Mills*

1298 (FOF 298)

Opposite top Lozells Road was served by the 69 bus route from the City Centre, which arrived in Lozells by way of Wheeler Street, an important local shopping centre that would be totally swept away in the 1960s Newtown redevelopment. In Lozells Road on 19 July 1951 is 1298; just one month later, this freshly overhauled bus was taken out of service and rebuilt by Leyland; fitted with an AEC pre-selector gearbox and Leyland 0350 engine, FOF 298 became a test-bed as Edinburgh Corporation's 185 in connection with the LH double-deck project, which would pave the way for the rear-engined 'Atlantean'. The bus is passing Buchan's chemist shop, next door to Mellow & Sons, provision merchants, but not necessarily grocers! Between the off-licence on the corner of Berners Street and the bus is a Bedford PC 15 cwt van, while travelling towards Wheeler Street on the city-bound 69 route is 2188 (JOJ 188), a 1950 Leyland 'Titan' PD2/1 with a Park Royal H29/25R body. *G. F. Douglas, courtesy of A. D. Packer*

1299 (FOF 299)

Middle After the abandonment of the Soho Road tram routes, the impressive shelters at the front of Snow Hill station were retained, being only about eight years old. FOF 299 is standing on the forecourt of Snow Hill when working on the 74 route in about February 1941. It is fully equipped with headlight masks and has white-painted mudguards and a camouflaged roof and rear dome. The bright winter sunlight dazzles off the side, but also reveals the recent effects of the bombing of Hockley Garage: between the decks around the front destination box, parts of the primrose livery have been freshly patched up. *C. F. Klapper*

1316 (FOF 316)

Bottom This bus was used in the official publicity photographs by Leyland Motors in the autumn of 1939, and on Saturday 3 June 1950 it is standing at the stops in Corporation Street between Lower Priory and Bull Street. By now the bulkhead in the half-cab area below the front lower saloon window was painted predominantly blue. FOF 316 is operating, fairly unusually, on a cross-city 29 service to Highfield Road, Hall Green, indicating that it was one of only a few of the class to be retained by Hockley Garage when the Ladywood tram service was replaced on 31 August 1947. Although this section of Corporation Street was one-way towards Bull Street from the distant Old Square, the tram tracks were used by trams going in the opposite direction from their individual termini in Martineau Street; the result was that trams going to Washwood Heath, Alum Rock and Perry Barr had to go against the flow of the

motor traffic. Passing the seven-storey Lewis's department store is 1626 (GOE 626), a Daimler CVG6 with an MCCW H30/24R body that entered service in February 1948. *G. F. Douglas, courtesy of A. D. Packer*

RT 19 (FXT 194)
AEC 'Regent' 0661 RT-type; AEC A185 9.6-litre engine; LPTB H30/26R body; es 1.1940

This bus, AEC's RT demonstrator, was demonstrated to BCT between 7 June and 7 July 1941. It was a standard London Transport RT-type with a composite-framed body constructed at Chiswick. It was painted in a lined-out green livery, but there is no known photograph of it demonstrating to Birmingham.

1320-1323 (FVP 920-923)
Daimler COG6; Gardner 6LW 8.4-litre engine; MCCW H32/26R body (Contract 239); es 12.1941-3.1942, w 9.1954

During the autumn of 1941 five Daimlers with Metro-Cammell bodies were built for Johannesburg in South Africa, but they were not exported because of German U-boat activity in the Atlantic. Four were allocated to BCT by the Ministry of War Transport, and the fifth became West Monmouth Omnibus Board's 20 (EAX 729). Being 8 feet wide, Birmingham's four were subject to width restrictions, and were also unable to pass beneath bridges less than 14ft 9in. Initially they were allocated to Yardley Wood Garage for the 18 route, but in 1946 they moved to Harborne to operate the 9 service, where the wide Broad Street and the wider Hagley Road could be easily negotiated by these broader than normal buses. When Quinton Garage opened on 30 October 1949, the four 'Jo'burgs' were also moved to the new premises.

1320 (FVP 920)

Below left When the Daimler COG6s were delivered they were painted in an unrelieved all-over grey. There was a small destination number box at the front and another over the rear platform; both were initially painted over, but later they were completely plated over, which just left the normal front two-line destination display. All the saloon windows had full-drop windows, ideal for the hot climate of South Africa, but 'not so hot' for Birmingham! Gradually they were altered so that they only opened about one-third. The first of the quartet, FVP 920, is standing at The Valley, Yardley Wood Road, on 13 September 1944, working on the 18A route. The buses were used initially on this inter-suburban service between Yardley Wood and Northfield because the fairly wide roads could cope with their extra width, although the tree-battered front nearside dome suggests that a bit more pruning along Bunbury Road might have been in order. The extra power of the 6LW engine must have been useful when they tackled steep hills such as Parson's Hill in Kings Norton, which was part of this 18 route. *L. W. Perkins*

1321, (FVP 921)

Below Working towards the city on the 9 route in 1954 in its full Birmingham livery, which seemed to have all the primrose and blue bands much wider than on pre-war stock, FVP 921 passes the tiny triangle of trees, flower beds and grass that still provides a quiet haven at the junction of Hagley Road and Sandon Road, which is behind the trees on the right. At the apex of the junction was a large Victorian fountain, and it was from here that the first regular motorised bus service was introduced in October 1903 using a single-deck 12-seater Mulliner with a 12hp Napier petrol engine. Following 1321 is a virtually new Midland Red Leyland-bodied Leyland 'Titan' PD2/12s bus, known as the LD8, working on the 132 service from Bewdley, which will terminate in Navigation Street just beyond the Queen's Hotel. *P. Tizard*

1322 (FVP 922)

Travelling away from the distant Town Hall in New Street is 1322 (FVP 922), still in its original grey livery and yet to have its small disused front number blind panelled over. It is overtaking 248 (EOG 248), a 1939-built Leyland 'Titan' TD6cs with a 52-seat Metro-Cammell body, working on the 16A service to Beauchamp Avenue in Handsworth Wood, although by this time it had a radiator route board showing the late-1939 extension to Hamstead, which had not yet been added to the destination blinds. It is June 1945, yet 1322 is working on the 24 route from Warstock, when these four buses were still not officially cleared to come into the City Centre on account of their extra 6-inch width.

They were fitted with a white steering wheel to signify that they were 8 feet wide, and although the Corporation did not purchase any 8-foot-wide buses until almost the dawn of the rear-engined era, the 'Jo'burgs' were influential in that their raked windscreen was adopted as the standard for all post-war exposed-radiatored buses. Also, although never used, was it a coincidence that the original destination box layout at the front was employed on all the 'new look'-front buses from February 1950 until October 1954? *F. W. York*

1324-1326 (FON 324-326)
Leyland 'Titan' TD7;
Leyland 8.6-litre diesel
engine; Leyland H30/26R
body; es 2.1942-5.1942,
w 4.1954-9.1954

These three buses were part of an order for Western Scottish Motor Traction that was stopped by the Ministry of War Transport in 1941; when they were 'unfrozen', or released for distribution, by the MoWT they were allocated to Birmingham in October 1941. The TD7 had replaced the TD5 chassis in late 1939 and was designed to have virtually no idling vibration, with a large flywheel that resulted in very slow gear changes. It would therefore have been best suited to long inter-urban company-operated

routes where gear changes were at a minimum, but in Birmingham they were mainly employed on the long Outer Circle 11 service or the cross-city 29A route. They were allocated to Perry Barr Garage for their entire career in Birmingham. and were delivered with grey paintwork.

1324 (FON 324)

The first of the 'unfrozen' TD7s, FON 324, is about to cross the Birmingham & Fazeley Canal as it leaves the Fort Dunlop factory, carrying workers away from the utility shelters in Holly Lane on 30 June 1953. It is working on the peak-hours-only 40 service to Lozells via Gravelly Hill, a new bus route that replaced the 5 tram route on 1 October 1950, the same day as the Washwood Heath and Alum Rock tram routes closed. As Birmingham was given no choice in the selection of vehicles, for the first time ('Jo'burgs' excepted) it was operating buses with a full 56-seat capacity, which was the standard almost everywhere else in the country. These attractive buses were not particularly liked by the drivers as they had terribly slow gear changes, which could be improved upon if the clutch stop was used, but after a long shift that was hard work! *Author's collection*

1327 (FON 327)
Leyland 'Titan' TD7; Leyland 8.6-litre diesel engine; Park Royal MoS H30/26R body; es 1.1942, w 12.1948

Thirteen 'unfrozen' TD7 buses were built with Park Royal 'utility' bodies; London Transport had 11 as its STD 101-111, Felix of Hatfield had EWR 423, and 1327 was the 13th. It carried the penultimate chassis number and penultimate body number, and was the second into service and the first one to be withdrawn. It was a Perry Barr bus for all of its short career.

1327 (FON 327)
The camera-shy FON 327 is being used on an 11 route shortworking in 1947 and is carrying a radiator slip-board for 'TYBURN ROAD'. It was delivered in wartime grey livery but had upholstered seats, although an unglazed upper saloon rear emergency window rather enhanced its wartime look. By 1947 it was in full fleet livery with a very deep cream-painted waistrail and a fully glazed top deck. *P. Tizard*

1328 (FON 628)
Leyland 'Titan TD7; Leyland 8.6-litre diesel engine; Northern Coach Builders MoS H30/26R body; es 6.1942, w 9.1949

NCB, based in Newcastle-upon-Tyne, only built a few wartime bus bodies on new chassis, and by 1944 was manufacturing a body that, in outline at least, looked like a peacetime one. This bus was allocated by the MoWT to BCT in October 1941 and was delivered with all-over grey paintwork. It had a height restriction, being too tall to pass beneath the bridges on the Inner Circle route which were plated at 14ft 6in.

1328 (FON 628)
The second wartime 'utility' bus to come to the undertaking was 1328 (FON 628), which is standing at the large wrought-iron bus shelters just below the junction with Hawthorn Road in Kingstanding Road on 31 July 1943, still in the all-over grey paintwork in which it was delivered during mid-June 1942, some eight months after it was allocated to the Corporation by the MoWT; it would have to wait until the end of hostilities before it was repainted into fleet colours. It is working into the city on the 33 route, which strangely not only operated all the eight new but slow-gear-change TD7s, but also had all the 'piano-front' AEC 'Regents' of 1929-31 that had been converted to run on producer gas. In the background is a Wrenson's grocery and provisions shop, one of the many retail premises around this junction. *L. W. Perkins*

1329-1331 (FON 629-631)
Leyland 'Titan' TD7; Leyland 8.6-litre diesel engine; Leyland H30/26R body; es 7.1942, w 9.1951-5.1954

These three buses were also destined for Western Scottish Motor Traction, but construction was stopped by the Ministry of War Transport in 1941, and, when they were 'unfrozen', they were allocated to Birmingham in October 1941, but with Duple 'utility' bodies. They were allocated to Perry Barr

Garage for their entire operational time in Birmingham, and were delivered with grey paintwork.

1329 (FON 629)
Opposite above In about 1951, 1329 (FON 629) has just completed loading with passengers while passing through Digbeth on the cross-city 29A route. With its very battered front nearside wing, it is at the bus stop alongside the waste ground on which Midland Red parked its Digbeth Garage allocation of buses. It is facing the steep climb up through

the Bull Ring, which the driver must face with a certain amount of trepidation knowing that he will have to use the clutch stop in order to achieve a quick gear change from the crash gearbox. *R. Marshall*

1330 (FON 630)

Below right Are the two gentlemen striding across Harborne Lane towards the Golden Cross public house going for a quick pint? Bus 1330, an 'unfrozen' all-Leyland TD7 with a body built to full peacetime standards despite not entering service until 17 July 1942, is working on the 11 route in about 1948, and is about to pull away up the steep rise leading into Harborne Park Road. Behind the bus is the row of ten 1920s-built shops in Harborne Lane just short of Quinton Road. FON 630 was eventually sold to Stevenson of Spath, who ran it for another 11 years before it was bought for preservation. Unfortunately the years have not been kind to it, and it now only survives as a chassis. What a wasted opportunity! *B. W. Ware*

ROUTE INDEX

This list shows all Birmingham's pre-war bus routes (together with some shown in *italics* that were post-war routes, but seen here being operated by pre-war buses). The majority of routes are illustrated in the book.